Siegfried Kracauer

Siegfried Kracauer

AN INTRODUCTION

Gertrud Koch

Translated by Jeremy Gaines

PRINCETON UNIVERSITY PRESS

PRINCETON, NEW JERSEY

Library of Congress Cataloging-in-Publication Data

Koch, Gertrud, 1949–
[Kracauer zur Einführung. English]
Siegfried Kracauer : an introduction / Gertrud Koch ;
translated by Jeremy Gaines.
p.   cm.
Includes bibliographical references and index.
ISBN 0-691-01613-5 (cloth : alk. paper). —
ISBN 0-691-04992-0 (pb : alk. paper)
1. Kracauer, Siegfried, 1889–1966—Criticism and interpretation.
2. Motion pictures.   3. Germany—Intellectual life—20th century.
I. Gaines, Jeremy.   II. Title.
PT2621.R135 Z7613   2000
834'.912—dc21   99-089189

This book has been composed in Bitstream Caledonia

Originally published as *Kracauer zur Einführung* © Junius Verlag, 1996.

The paper used in this publication meets the minimum requirements
of ANSI/NISO Z39.48-1992 (R1997) (*Permanence of Paper*)

www.pup.princeton.edu

Printed in the United States of America

1   2   3   4   5   6   7   8   9   10

1   2   3   4   5   6   7   8   9   10
(pbk.)

Contents

Preface

USUALLY, introductions are written about those authors (and works) who have been so widely discussed that a summarizing overview of the various interpretations of his or her work appears desirable. It would therefore seem high time to introduce readers to Siegfried Kracauer the author. Having said this, it is still too early to write an introduction. This book can only claim to be a provisional attempt. Although the collected edition of his works is not yet complete, his estate, housed in the Marbach Literary Archive near Stuttgart, is well cataloged, and on both sides of the Atlantic there have been significant attempts to bring Kracauer out from behind the shadows cast by his friends of the Frankfurt School.

About a decade ago I held a seminar where I presented texts by Kracauer and I later mentioned the course to Leo Lowenthal, a close friend of his. Lowenthal, who was at the time besieged by scholars writing histories of the Frankfurt School, was somewhat astonished. He had hardly imagined that his friend "Friedel" would suddenly emerge as a big name on the academic scene. Years later it was he who opened one of the very first conferences devoted to Kracauer, held at Columbia University. Yet the distance with which the friends of his youth in Frankfurt eventually treated Kracauer's work was still evident in Lowenthal's response. With the benefit of hindsight, distances can shrink into differences within a common overall project. The room that Kracauer has been allocated in the Frankfurt School is sparse. There are, however, other reasons, too, why I am not quite clear whether Kracauer was ever really at home in it or whether in some phases of his life he would not have liked to take his seat there. Kracauer's notion of "exterritoriality" can perhaps magically be brought to bear here; yet he did not have much more or much less luck than others associated with the Frankfurt School. The extent to which he distanced himself from it can be gleaned from his own writings. The historians and philologists will do their part in measuring what joint space these thinkers occupied and will then be able to reassess it, invoking the inheritance of the Frankfurt School in his name, too.

I by no means wish to take part in this Brechtian Caucasian Circle into which Kracauer has been dragged, like Benjamin before him. To my mind, not only the zeal of battling critics, but also the contents of his works are responsible for such a circle having been chalked around him. With all due respect, his oeuvre is not borne by some systematic philosophical construction, but instead lives from many, often highly contradictory motifs. They are mainly held together by one thing: his name. And I mean this quite literally. Kracauer's texts, his philosophical treatises, his essays, reviews, and glosses are all linked by a literary style that weaves them into one infinite, simultaneous fabric. Their precise literary character allows us, indeed compels us, to interpret them by studying the rhetoric of the metaphors rather than the structure of the concepts.

Introductions tend to presume that the primary texts of an author form a canonical body and then reconstruct them in as elegant a manner as possible. In the case of the present book, I have inverted this strategy. I am interested more in revealing Kracauer's qualities through the texts themselves and their specific literary substance. For this reason, I wish to nurture the same enthusiasm for his novels as exists for those pieces of his extensive oeuvre that are already canonized, namely his analyses of film, his history of film, and his theory of film. These already have a firm place in film studies, even if they are often completely misunderstood or sharply rejected.

Time Line of Kracauer's Life

1889   Born on 8 February in Frankfurt, the only child of Rosette
        and Adolf Kracauer.
1898   Enters high school at the Philanthropin, Frankfurt.
1904   Moves to the Klinger Upper High.
1907   Graduates; in August, his first article for the arts section of
        Frankfurter Zeitung appears. The same year he starts
        studying architecture at the nearby Polytechnic in Darm-
        stadt.
1908–9 Continues his studies at the Berlin Polytechnic and gradu-
        ates from the Munich Polytechnic.
1911   Works in an architect's office; travels, writes literary
        pieces, prepares his Ph.D. thesis, *Die Entwicklung der
        Schmiedekunst in Berlin, Potsdam und einigen Städten der
        Mark vom 17. Jahrhundert bis zum Beginn des 19. Jahr-
        hunderts.*
1914   His thesis is accepted in Berlin and published by Worm-
        ser Verlags- und Druckereigesellschaft in 1915. With the
        outbreak of World War One, he returns to Frankfurt and
        works in an architect's office.
1916   Takes part in a competition for a Soldiers' Memorial Cem-
        etery, which he wins; first contact with Max Scheler.
1917   Called up to the artillery in Mainz.
1918   Employed as an architect in Osnabrück; death of his
        father; returns to Frankfurt. While earning money as an
        architect, he writes philosophical studies. At his family's
        behest, he befriends Theodor Adorno (and, in 1920, Leo
        Lowenthal).
1919   Completes a study on his teacher in Berlin, *Georg
        Simmel. Ein Beitrag zur Deutung des geistigen Lebens
        unserer Zeit* (Georg Simmel: A contribution to an inter-
        pretation of the intellectual life of his times).
1920   Occasional work as an architect.
1921   Receives a permanent freelance appointment at the *Frank-

furter Zeitung. Many of his important essays begin to appear there. Makes the acquaintance of Rabbi Nobel and Franz Rosenzweig.

1922   Soziologie als Wissenschaft (Sociology as science) is published. Starts writing Der Detektiv-Roman (The detective novel). Travels with his friends Adorno and Lowenthal. Gets to know Ernst Bloch, contact with whom was broken off for several years following Kracauer's critical review of Bloch's book on Thomas Münster.

1924   In November, appointed editor at Frankfurter Zeitung.

1925   Starts writing his novel Ginster.

1926   Meets his future wife Elisabeth (Lili) Ehrenreich, a librarian at the Frankfurt Institute for Social Research. Kracauer's criticism of the Buber-Rosenzweig translation of the Old Testament leads to a change in his circle of friends. Reconciled with Bloch but rejected first by Margarete Susman and then by Buber.

1927   The Mass Ornament appears, as does the essay "Photography." Travels to Paris and France.

1928   Ginster is published, first serialized in Frankfurter Zeitung, then as a book by S. Fischer Verlag.

1929   Starts working on a new novel, Georg, which he later completes in exile.One chapter comes out in advance.

1930   Die Angestellten appears in a series of twelve sections in Frankfurter Zeitung and is then published by Frankfurter Societäts-Druckerei. Kracauer and Lili Ehrenreich marry and move to Berlin, where Kracauer joins the local editorial team of Frankfurter Zeitung.

1931–33 Conditions at the paper deteriorate. Kracauer writes articles against the Ufa and its increasingly nationalistic film productions.

1933   On 28 February, one day after the Reichstag Fire, the Kracauers leave for Paris. Struggles to get work both as a journalist and from his old friends from Frankfurt. Contact with Benjamin.

1934   Completes his second novel Georg. Starts work on his book on Offenbach.

1935   Finishes *Offenbach*, a study that prompts sharp criticism from Adorno.

1936   Is commissioned with smaller jobs by New York for the New School for Social Research and the Frankfurt Institute in exile. Prepares to emigrate to the United States.

1937   At the end of the year, the necessary affidavit arrives. Receives an offer to write a study on the social history of German film for the Library of the Museum of Modern Art. The project eventually results in *From Caligari to Hitler*. At the outbreak of the war, is interned for two months near Paris with other emigrants from Germany. Released after people backing him intervene.

1940   Again interned and then released. Flees, despite great risk, to Marseilles, where he again encounters Benjamin.

1941   The Kracauers manage to get through Spain to Portugal. Renewed difficulties in Lisbon. At the end of April, Lili and Siegfried Kracauer disembark in New York.

1941–45   Begins work as assistant to Iris Barry at the Library of the Museum of Modern Art, working on *From Caligari to Hitler*. He spends the next few years compiling studies on commission, including *Propaganda and the Nazi War Film* and *The Conquest of Europe on the Screen—The Nazi Newsreel, 1939–1940*. Work becomes increasingly empirical.

1946   Becomes a U.S. citizen.

1947   *From Caligari to Hitler* is published by Princeton University Press, with help from Erwin Panofsky.

1949   Begins work on *Theory of Film*, with the material assistance of a stipend. Notes made in Marseilles provide the foundation for the book. Begins to concern himself with psychology.

1950   Works under commission for Voice of America. While writing the book on film aesthetics, he gradually develops a reputation as a specialist for empirical social research.

1951   Appointed Research Director of the Empirical Social Research Department at Columbia University. Works with Paul Lazarsfeld.

1952 His essay on "qualitative content analysis" is published. Through 1955 he focuses entirely on empirical studies and organizing research programs.

1956 Returns to *Theory of Film*.

1959 Finishes *Theory of Film*. Makes his first trips back to Europe and undertakes various empirical studies.

1960–66 Devises the plan for his book on history. Travels to Europe. Draws up plans for an edition of his widespread and scattered works.

1966 Spends the summer months in Europe. In New York he falls ill and dies of pneumonia on 26 November.

Siegfried Kracauer

The Early Days:
A Biographical Sketch

SIEGFRIED KRACAUER is one of those authors to whom that sad saying applies: his fame is nothing more than "the sum of errors" connected with his name. Under his name we would find Harold Bloom's fictitious "map of misreading" with all the possible contradictory but also productive interpretations and with all the unproductive misunderstandings that have tended to get in the way. Most prominent among these are some theorists of film who wish to do their best to punish the name Kracauer for having produced a naive apology for realism, without actually having understood the philosophical construction on which his phenomenology of film rests.

As a consequence, cycles of readings have come and gone. The reception of Kracauer still stands on unsteady feet, to the extent that it stands at all. And things are made difficult by the fact that his name has been entered on various topographical maps. Kracauer exists either as a film theorist or as a distant relative of the Frankfurt School, either as a journalist or as a philosopher, either as an essay-writer or as a novelist. In ironic desperation, Kracauer therefore once asked in a letter penned on the occasion of a preface that was to be attached to one of his books, not to be presented as a "film man," but instead as "a philosopher of culture, or also as a sociologist, and as a poet. . . . With regard to film, it has always only been a hobby I pursued in order to make certain sociological and philosophical statements."[1]

Seen from a distance, we can discern a pattern in the various maps readers have made of the author's work and the divergent interpretations they have come up with. The pattern, although it has a shape of its own, can be understood as an extension of his work—or as a "constitutive surface," to use Kracauer's own concept.

If we assume that the "constitutive surface" of Kracauer's oeuvre is a structure in its own right, then we will find it easier to comprehend the internal fissures and outstanding characteristics of the individual writings. Indeed, anyone who is at a loss when confronted by Kracauer's writings—unable to decide whether he should approach Kracauer the film theorist, Kracauer the philosopher, Kracauer the poet, or Kracauer the journalist with a view to grasping the man's thought—will be unable to see the structural identity of these different parts. Right through to his last book, Kracauer adhered to the idea of a compositional principle behind a surface which itself had no center; it was on this surface that he tried to depict both micro- and macro-structures. A page from the manuscript version of the table of contents in that last book, *History: The Last Things before the Last*, for example, states that the first point must be an "Emphasis on minutiae—microanalysis—Close-up." Kracauer then cuts from the technical "long shot" to philosophical concepts such as "Progress" or "Dialectics."[2] This mixture would appear to be significant, combining both an aesthetic form of representation (e.g., the close-up) and a conceptual presentation based around abstract categories. However, Kracauer places the latter in a context he calls the "web of interpretation" in a handwritten addendum to the manuscript. In the same draft, we find a potential chapter 14 titled "Theological (and philosophical) views—lurking around the corner."[3] What lurks around the corner is not only his intellectual heritage, but also a linguistic reference to his preference for images and to his vivid language, on which his fame as a journalist rested. That the manuscript in question was purely a preliminary sketch later fleshed out further and revised by hand indicates that the writer moved in such striking linguistic images in daily life. In other words, this trait is not just the stylistic finesse of the printed work but a way of thinking.

If one were to assess Kracauer's oeuvre after the fact to discover its internal consistency by separating out the different language games (such as the literary or philosophical), one would fail to uncover the unique character of Kracauer's work. This mixture of linguistic systems has for too long obscured a clear view of his oeuvre and instead has created a somewhat hapless subdivision of the research on his thought. He has been studied only in terms of the narrow confines of a particular discipline. Film theorists have come up against the limits of their profession, but so have the philosophers who suspected Kracauer of playing linguistic games on them.

In the above-cited letter, with its recommendations on how best to present his own person, Kracauer asks his biographer not to mention the date of his birth. He may have feared that the fixed point given by the objectivity of a date would cause too much weight to be attached to the subjectivity of his person and would cause the author to pale like an old photograph. In the course of his life, which was not exactly lacking in bitter disappointments and rejection, Kracauer, the author of extraterritoriality, was only too aware that his oeuvre begged mis-understandings. These stemmed from the deliberate choice of differ-ent subject matters, as he suggests in the introduction to "History: The Last Things before the Last," which took up themes that had also been treated in the older "Theory of Film":

> This book which I had always conceived as an aesthetics of the photo-graphic media, not less and not more, now that I have penetrated the veil that envelops one's most intimate endeavors, appears to me in its true light: as another attempt of mine to bring out the significance of areas whose claim to be acknowledged in their own right has not yet been recognized. I say "another attempt" because this was what I had tried to do throughout my life—in *Die Angestellten*, perhaps in *Ginster*, and cer-tainly in the *Offenbach*. So at long last all my main efforts, so incoherent on the surface, fall into line—they all have served, and continue to serve, a single purpose: the rehabilitation of objectives and modes of being which still lack a name and hence are overlooked or misjudged. Perhaps this is less true of history than of photography; yet history too marks a bent of the mind and defines a region of reality which despite all that has been written about them are still largely *terra incognita*.[4]

Here, Kracauer himself outlines the reasons for one of the various obstacles that a "proper" reception of his work has had to overcome. Like Walter Benjamin, Kracauer casts the gaze of a flaneur on the surface, construing the latter as a system of information, a new social text, which many jointly write and only a very few read. As a con-sequence, even in his early writings we find a phenomenological in-terpretation of the everyday world of modernity. He thus placed things that were ostensibly close at hand at a great distance; for exam-ple, under his pen the physical proximity of the "Tiller girls" gels to form an abstract ornament, which readers are expected to understand as a sign. It is quite easy to see in such figures of thought the old phenomenological agenda, but Kracauer's actual interest is in reading the world of objects contemplated as a picture, in terms of an ideology critique. This dual structure of knowledge—as contemplation and interpretation—links Kracauer to more recent issues in film theory.

The dual structure can also be found from an early date in the intellectual development of Siegfried Kracauer, who started his professional life in the first decade of the twentieth century as both an architect and novelist, as well as in the family into whose midst he was born on February 8, 1889, in Frankfurt on Main. His father Adolf claims to have become a businessman because, by choosing a practical profession, he enabled his younger brother Isidor to study. The two brothers eventually married sisters in Frankfurt, Rosette and Hedwig Oppenheimer. From earliest childhood, Siegfried spent his days not just with his parents, but also with his Uncle Isidor and Aunt Hedwig. In keeping with his mother's wish, Isidor Kracauer had embarked on studies at the Theological Faculty in Wroclaw with the goal of becoming a rabbi.

However, Isidor allowed himself to be swayed by his interest in secular studies, specifically in history. In so doing, he made a name for himself, not as a rabbi, but instead as a teacher at the Philanthropin, the Jewish high school in Frankfurt. Founded by the Frankfurt Jewish community to promote schooling in the humanities, and open to both Jews and Gentiles, the Philanthropin brought together an enlightened group of people who were interested in theological issues. It was to this group that Siegfried Kracauer often implicitly referred in his writings. His uncle Isidor, who taught history at the school for over forty years, also undertook research into regional Jewish history. This culminated in his two-volume *Zur Geschichte der Juden in Frankfurt am Main 1150–1824* (On the history of the Jews in Frankfurt on Main, 1150–1824), which is to this day considered a standard work on the uncertain fate of the Jewish community in Frankfurt. Siegfried would undoubtedly have been encouraged in numerous ways by his uncle, and it was to him that Siegfried wrote high-spirited letters while vacationing. Shortly after finishing high school in 1907, Kracauer's first article appeared in *Frankfurter Zei-*

tung, and he commenced studying architecture in Darmstadt the very same year. He studied there as well as in Berlin and Munich, where he finally graduated in 1911.

Parallel to his practical work as an architect, he continued pursuing his study of philosophical, sociological, and epistemological questions—an interest sparked during his student days. He was captivated, above all, by Kant's theory of cognition. It would be easy to conclude from Kracauer's studies and short professional career as an architect that he had some special talent and inclination for spatial thought and imagination. One source of proof is his Ph.D. thesis, completed in 1914, *Die Entwicklung der Schmiedekunst in Berlin, Potsdam und einigen Städten der Mark vom 17. Jahrhundert bis zum Beginn des 19. Jahrhunderts* (On the development of the art of smithry in Berlin, Potsdam and several towns in the March, from the seventeenth century until the beginning of the nineteenth century), which is an example of his intense focus on ornament. However, the first jobs he got in architectural offices were not exactly inspiring and were relatively short-lived.

When the Great War broke out, he returned to Frankfurt and started writing before he found a new job with an architectural firm. In 1916, he designed a memorial cemetery for soldiers. In *Ginster*, his autobiographical novel, he described the layout:

> The general times of war . . . called for a layout in which the horrors of war were repeated. Instead of using the previous sketches, Ginster therefore applied his set square and ruler to manufacturing a cemetery system that resembled a military flow chart. . . . Laid out according to strictly scientific principles, open to all members of the public. Rectangular graveyards were aligned to a central square, on which the memorial rose upwards like a superior officer. It consisted of an elevated cube, crowned by several slabs. Three sides of the cube were to be used for the names of the dead, while the fourth was to bear a motto. . . . The monument looked down on its troops as if stopping to watch them parade; indeed, not the slightest irregularity was to be seen."[5]

In 1917, Kracauer was conscripted into an artillery unit in Mainz; it was a complex experience that he shared along with most of his generation—who enthused about the war. In *Ginster*, the successfully designed structure of 1916 gives way to an edifice analyzed with great coldness and distance, and is critically altered. It reflects the experience of life in a conurbation, of modern architecture as part of an overall plan for life in which even questions of style become social ciphers.

After the war, it proved difficult to find a new job. Kracauer increasingly worked as a reviewer for *Frankfurter Zeitung*, becoming editor of the arts section in 1921. It was about then that he first met members of the future Frankfurt School; he became close friends, above all, with Theodor Adorno and Leo Lowenthal. These friendships lasted for the rest of his life, even if Kracauer never belonged to the inner circle of people associated with the Frankfurt Institute for Social Research. Later, when in exile in the United States, Leo Lowenthal and Siegfried Kracauer closed ranks, even if in the final analysis they stood for different philosophical positions.

Until moving to Berlin, his last stop before taking the arduous road to exile, Kracauer was essentially influenced by Frankfurt intellectual life, if we ignore brief periods of study in Munich and Berlin. And in particular he was inspired by the thought that was prevalent in the Yeshiva, where Rabbis Nobel, Rosenzweig, and Buber (who passed through) did not fail to make an impact on Kracauer and Lowenthal, despite Kracauer's later sharp critique of Rosenzweig and Buber's new translation of the Bible.[6] Many years later, Adorno, who studied Kant with Kracauer on Saturdays, remembered above all the idiosyncratic and convincing introduction Kracauer gave his young friend. In his famous essay on Kracauer, Adorno described these study sessions and the Kant interpretation that they resulted in:

> I may be qualified to make a start on this . . . by outlining some of the features of the figure of Kracauer: he and I have been friends since I was a young man. I was a student at the *Gymnasium* when I met him near the end of the First World War. A friend of my parents, Rosie Stern, had invited the two of us to her house. She was a tutor at the Philanthropin, where Kracauer's uncle, the historiographer of the Frankfurt Jews, was a member of the faculty. . . .
>
> For years, Kracauer read the "Critique of Pure Reason" regularly on Saturday afternoon with me. I am not exaggerating in the slightest when

I say that I owe more to this reading than to my academic teachers. . . . Under his guidance I experienced the work from the beginning not as mere epistemology, not as an analysis of the conditions of scientifically valid judgments, but as a kind of coded text from which the historical situation of spirit could be read, with the vague expectation that in doing so one could acquire something of truth itself. . . .

Without being able to account for it fully, through Kracauer I perceived for the first time the expressive moment in philosophy: putting into words the thoughts that come into one's head.[7]

Many years later, his old friend Leo Lowenthal was to vouch for the fact that Kracauer was an unusual intellectual. Lowenthal described him as one of those thinkers who found the role of "thorn" or "debunker" more appropriate than that of prophet or soothsayer: "As a critic he always maintained, I would say, an attitude of extreme commitment and, at the same time, a constant unwillingness to surrender to any absolutes; he always raised doubts, always retained this critical attitude. In this sense he was really a super-member of our school of critical thinking."[8]

His recalcitrant insistence on critique did not only make him friends; it also destroyed the friendly relations of others. Lowenthal, for example, reports that following Kracauer's sharp critique of Buber and Rosenzweig, and Rosenzweig's equally vehement reaction, he had to put his own friendship with Buber at risk when standing by Kracauer.[9]

As early as 1921, Kracauer composed an essay titled "On Friendship," in which he made all sorts of clever distinctions in order to dissect the different forms of human relationships.[10] The combination of analytical categories and phenomenological observations already attests to Kracauer's feel for psychological detail, something that may have been the product of his early study of those philosophers who wrote on the subconscious emotions of the soul.

On finally abandoning architecture as a profession and joining the editorial staff of *Frankfurter Zeitung* in 1921, he was already thirty-two years old. On emigrating to France in 1933, he was in his mid-forties. On disembarkation in New York in 1941 (where he was met by his old friend from Frankfurt, Lowenthal), he was fifty-two and faced the awesome prospect of having to start a new life and find a new way of making a living and new friends. In the 1920s, as a witty gesture, he had sent Lowenthal and Adorno a letter posted from the "headquarters of the transcendental homeless."[11] Now, it looked dangerously as if he had gone ashore precisely at that headquarters.

The Early Phenomenology
of Modernity and Mass Culture:
Of Hotel Lobbies and Detective Novels

COMMENTATORS tend to regard Kracauer's notion of the "surface" as the key theme in his thinking. If we follow this thread in his thought, we soon see that the concept is again by no means univocal. It is fair to say that the "surfaces" Kracauer describes exhibit innate breaking points, built into them at the theoretical level by the phenomenology of his approach. He does not construe the surface as an objective reality in the sense of the reality the natural sciences claim to describe. Instead, the surface confronts the transcendental subject of epistemology as a "reality stripped of meaning." The modern individual, divided from both the world and nature in the course of secularization, has to redefine himself and is, in turn, redefined by the process of societalization.

In his essay "Sociology as Science," drafted in 1920 and published in 1922, Kracauer takes his cue from Edmund Husserl and endeavors to formulate a theory of cognition with reference to the emergence of modern science. He writes: "Not until the world divides into a reality stripped of meaning, on the one hand, and the subject, on the other, does the latter fall prey to evaluating reality or investigating its being, to elucidating universal laws underlying occurrences, or to grasping, describing and interrelating in some way the occurrences which he experiences as discrete events."[1]

Kracauer assumes an a priori division of subject and world, and then takes this as the basis for the standpoint informing cognition. At the same time, he stresses the process of subjectification involved, affirming that "depending on the intention with which the Ego approaches reality," the appearance of reality changes.[2] What strikes the eye here is how Kracauer again develops a conceptual edifice using the three-dimensional notions of an architect.

11

Kracauer believes there are two sciences applicable to the "world of socialized man". First, there is *history*, the science that essays to understand the individual occurrences and their irreversible temporal sequence. Then there is *sociology*, which addresses those "laws" that emerge from socialization itself.

Although his treatise is written in a somewhat terse, academic style and hardly attests to the talents he had as a master of fiction, it once again reveals the doubts Kracauer has when it comes to the advantages of the two formal schools of philosophy that evidently impress him most. For he offers a materialist objection to both Kant's concept of the transcendental subject and the notions of pure phenomenology. Although he concedes that a reading of Husserl's ontology in line with Kant's formalism could provide the conceptual underpinnings for a formal sociology, he immediately demurs that although "of compelling evidentiality throughout," knowledge gained in this manner entirely fails to address its material object. He notes: "Starting from this knowledge, the task at hand must be to reconstruct overall social reality in sociological terms—and precisely when faced by this task Kant's transcendental subject and the pure Ego of phenomenology fail at the logical level."[3]

In a move intended as a critique of the scholarly disciplines as they existed at that time, Kracauer distinguishes between sociology, on the one hand, and the "empty spaces" of formal philosophy and the pure empirical matter of, for example, psychology, on the other. What he has in mind is to defend sociology as a heuristic procedure in order to use it as a diagnostic tool:

> Without in individual cases pointing beyond experience, it [sociology] allows us to identify regularities that can definitely be validated empirically and then be assessed—once we rid ourselves of the manic idea that they are directly based on the necessity of empty space. Indeed, a knowledge of such regularities to a certain degree enables us to predict future shapes taken by the respective constitution of social diversity. In fact, we would perhaps be correct to attach greater import to the practical edge of such a material-sociological conceptual future than to its decidedly theoretical benefits as a source of truth.[4]

In other words, while Kracauer takes the debate on the theoretical status of sociology seriously, he then qualifies its value. We should not forget that his indictment refers to a debate that is hardly plausible today—namely whether sociology can be based on a formal theory of truth or not. This would assume that sociology concerns itself with objects that we can meaningfully state are either true or false.

Although Kracauer explicitly points out that sociology cannot exist without the stuff of empiricism, he is sufficiently farsighted to add a Kantian constructivism to the empirical side of sociology. At the same time, he asserts that the objective side of sociology is impervious to the deductions of systems of transcendental philosophy. In the final analysis, this prompts him to take what is essentially a hermeneutic stance. And this approach cautiously supports the heuristic thrust of sociological thinking to the extent that it allows diagnostic generalizations. Quite in keeping with his day, Kracauer believes that recording concrete matter, identifying individual detail, is something that should take the place of a more stringently empirical approach. We could, in fact, say that Kracauer tries ironically to sidestep the debate of the time on whether sociology was a science—by prophetically pointing to the traces clearly left by the individual phenomena. Even if the "constructs" of a presumed reality enable us virtually to "go freely beyond" these, he is well aware that such a strategy can hardly get by without relying on a philosophy of history, even if the latter is only meant to supplement the "material-sociological" considerations.

Evidently, Kracauer is of the opinion that the overall outline of the course things take over time remains hidden from our view—all we see are the traces it has left. Kracauer states of his method: "The empirical-sociological procedure is naturally unable to afford an overview of the flow of time, let alone stop it. Proceeding from individual (randomly selected) points of diversity, as it were, it always only describes precisely those individual points; it can never cover the entire reach of reality."[5]

What we see rudimentarily here is one of the methods by means of which Kracauer gave his major essays such a cutting edge. Starting with individual observations and phenomena, he collects evidence without ever attempting to join it all up to form an overall picture. Kracauer's *Soziologie als Wissenschaft* (Sociology as Science) is his only study that is systematic in character. And perhaps it is logical that it is therefore perhaps one of his most unappealing. Yet, we can nevertheless elicit from it how he makes use of combined observation and interpretation as a basis on which to offer a diagnosis of contemporary society. At the time of its writing, he still shared his Frankfurt friends' critique of the schism between systematic philosophy and empiricism, of the dubious epistemological notion of the individual as somehow in no manner determined by historical and material preconditions. However, in his critique of scientific sociology he does not outline *avant la lettre* the integrative shape of a social theory that once more construes philosophy and individual sciences together, an attempt that took pride of place in the theoretical agenda of critical theory of the Frankfurt School only a few years later. In his later critical occupation with Georg Simmel and Max Weber he was loath to regard sociology as a field not ensnared in antinomies and paradoxes. Perhaps this indicates just how much his own strength did indeed lie in illuminating "individual points." The lines connecting the points remain virtual; that is to say, the space between them is not underscored to form a coherent picture. To a certain extent, Kracauer thus develops a form of pointillism, which, while locating all the dots or details at the joint level of the surface, does not link them up to forge causal chains.

Inka Mülder-Bach is surely right to criticize "Sociology as Science" for not having been up to the standard of sociology in its day. After all, sociology at the time Kracauer was writing already quite manifestly reflected on itself and was certainly not to be measured simply against the inherent contradictions of systematic philosophy. She correctly emphasizes that Kracauer insisted on the validity of the individual phenomenon in order to establish a bastion against "pure sociology": "Behind the roundabout justifications he gives for a 'pure sociology' and its juxtaposition to empirical matter, it is hard to see what Kracauer actually intends with this treatise. For his goal is to highlight the problems of systematic abstract theoretical orders which alienate thought from real-life phenomena to the extent that such orders cannot be referred to some specific reality."[6]

An age which had itself been brought about by the crisis in philosophy was obsessed with a yearning for the concrete—for material phenomena, for the objects of the empirical world, and for the experiences that could be made in it. It was no coincidence that psychology was considered the discipline in which the empiricism of the natural sciences and the heuristic-hermeneutic interpretative method of the cultural sciences appeared to merge. The gestalt psychology championed by psychology professors whose seminars Adorno and Horkheimer attended in Frankfurt is probably the clearest link connecting the different branches of phenomenology, neo-Kantianism, and empiricism. On the other hand, in 1919 the first German chair of sociology had been created at Frankfurt University—as a professorship for Franz Oppenheimer, a socialist—with special funding provided by a foundation.

We can assume that Kracauer, while following these developments at close quarters, did not feel himself particularly attached to the materialist thrust of sociology as represented, for example, by the Marxist approach promulgated by Karl Grüneburg at the Frankfurt Institute of Social Research. At any rate, little in *Soziologie als Wissenschaft* would suggest that he was. Instead, we can sense there something of the emphatic appeal of the writings of Freiburg philosopher Heidegger—at that time Husserl's assistant. Horkheimer, who was still majoring in psychology and was naturally also interested in Husserl's phenomenology, wrote to his bride-to-be with great enthusiasm in 1921: "What we must seek are not formal epistemological laws, for these are essentially unimportant. What we require are material statements on our lives and the meaning of it."[7] This agenda likewise held true for Kracauer, even if he expressed himself less radically.

Incidentally, we find a critique fueled by a study of Nietzsche among Kracauer's diary entries dating from his days as a student. He noted on August 18, 1912:

> Philosophy as science! This needs first to be debated thoroughly. Science, in other words a system of universal truths, accessible to all, logical, and not regarded emotionally. This presumes a hypothesis which must first be proved, namely that there is *an* aesthetic, *an* ethic, and *an* ideationally predefined path down which we travel ever further thanks to the common endeavor of generations. So many unproved suppositions lie in the ostensibly objective presumptions of academic philosophy![8]

After his detour into sociology, Kracauer compiled a "philosophical tractatus," which is what the subtitle of the study named *Der*

Detektiv-Roman ('The detective novel") claims the book to be. The
treatise is dedicated to "Theodor W. Adorno, my friend." Begun in
1922 and completed in 1925, only the chapter "The Hotel Lobby" was
ever published during Kracauer's lifetime, namely in the collection of
essays that came out as *The Mass Ornament*. The treatise as a whole
brings together almost all the themes of significance to Kracauer in
his early work. This is also true of the discernible emphasis on the
religious and theological spheres in his thought.

Kracauer starts with a reference to the spheres—by which he
means the "higher" and "religious" spheres defined in the Kierke-
gaardian sense of a theologically inspired existential philosophy. Indeed, in the first section of *Der Detektiv-Roman* Kracauer makes use
of Kierkegaard's concept of the "median being," the position occupied by humans between the spheres of "nature" and "super-nature."
Humans, as far removed from the natural state as they are from the
"higher" sphere of God, lead an existence defined just as much by
given things and occurrences as by a knowledge of the word of An-
nunciation and Revelation.

Inka Mülder-Bach has elaborated on the differences between Kracauer and Kierkegaard even at those junctures where Kracauer is a
faithful interpreter of Kierkegaard. She rightly points out that Kracauer tends to think more in terms of a topographical model, as was
common in medieval philosophy, and far less in terms of the "self-
reference" introduced by existential philosophical with its hierarchy
of spheres.[9] In existential philosophy, humans, as median beings, are
assumed by dint of this self-reference to have a double sense for reality. It is not sufficient for humans to consider the absolute as something that exists before them merely in the reified guise of *objects* of
thought. Such a view places humans solely in the role of observers.
Instead, the requirements of the higher spheres also have to be taken
into account in human existence. In other words, a paradox and tense
interim domain emerges between the spheres—and humans are
human precisely because they inhabit this domain.

Starting from this assumed interim domain, Kracauer sets out to
analyze the phenomenon of the detective novel as a "translation" of
human existence. Needless to say, what makes Kracauer's study so
exciting is less his use of Kierkegaard's notion of the "unconditional"

and more his rereading of Kierkegaard through the medium of a popular literary genre. Kracauer tries to prove by means of a philosophical argument that the status of the detective novel as a literary genre can be transformed. In this context, he identifies "disfigurement" as the sign of the "infinite process." He refers to disfigurement as a trope specific to the genre: the shrouding of revelation, that is the loss of the "name" in which the secret resides. He writes that

> the evidence of the high sphere remains inexorably in force. The form in which the evidence is disfigured reveals the higher spheres—although the disfigurement does not signify the higher spheres as such, for in the opaque medium things appear refracted, like the image of the rod dripped in water, and all names are distorted to the point where they are unrecognizable. . . . There are correspondences in the higher sphere for the muddled insights and attitudes of the lower regions—the knowledge they offer inauthentically provides the basis for authentic knowledge. These distorted images first become translucent when projected onto the substance distorted by them: If their meaning is to be liberated from its shrouds, they must be transformed until they reemerge in the coordinates of the system entailed by the higher sphere, where their meaning can be assessed.[10]

Kracauer's agenda for ideology critique is, in other words, informed by the theme of "disfigurement," and this notion of disfigurement can first be understood against the background of "revelation," a background that remains opaque. The "disfigurement" conceals the meaning of the "distorted images." Kracauer's goal in his study of the detective novel is to "retranslate" these images—that is, above all to reconstruct the paradoxes they contain. He terms the study an "interpretation," an "example of the art of translation," "which must actually prove that the one, the identical, which is directly lived by people in the relationship in question, . . . is reflected, however distortedly."[11] Put differently, Kracauer's version of a "redemptive critique" contains a theological strand that derives from the figure of revelation, under the spell of which even the "nameless" remain bound in their "disfigurement." Kracauer has an approach that is astonishingly egalitarian, addressing all the phenomena of the "lower culture" just as seriously as those of the "higher"; to his mind the former phenomena are all traces that point back to the "higher spheres" of Creation. And it is no coincidence that this assumption originates in a notion of equality that can be linked back to the idea of a God and a Law. Nevertheless, it would be overly one-sided to reduce Kracauer's trope of "revelatory" critique entirely to an underlying theological argument. Such a reading would be reductive and would provide a one-sided resolution of the paradoxical construct Kracauer outlines. We shall therefore for the time being defer answering the question whether a paradoxical figure must not necessarily eventually be resolved by a theological or metaphysical argument. Instead, we will focus on the twofold analysis Kracauer offers with his reading of the "secret" of the detective novel as an allusion to the metaphysical human condition.

After all, nothing other than the "Law" forms the unconditional, the "higher" sphere of the detective novel. Community is constructed by the Law, of which there are again two paradoxically related versions:

> Like the extant individual, the community to which he is allocated is in a paradoxical situation. . . . The paradox of this "interim state" corresponds to the ambiguity of the "Law" that governs the community. Now, we can assume that humans live so closely together that the Law seems to recede and love unites only those who have divested themselves of the Law. However, precisely the interim position of mankind provides a space for the external and the baser, dragging the Law down with it until such a time as salvation comes. The position whereby things becomes fixed, to the extent that it belongs to the realm of the conditional, must constantly be dissolved; to the extent that it is credulously received, the interrelational quality remains inalienably in force.[12]

What is interesting about Kracauer's concept of an interim state is his theological elucidation of the notion of Law, which he uses to link the detective novel and theology. Like his friend Walter Benjamin (in the latter's 1921 essay "Critique of Violence"), Kracauer also appends an adage by Anatole France in order to pinpoint the paradoxical structure involved. Benjamin had distinguished between three levels of violence, above all in order to address the question of justice and power. First, there is mythical force such as sets down the law (which Benjamin terms the "law-making" function). Second, there is the force that serves the first and thus to preserve the law, the "law-preserving" function. Finally there is "divine power," which Benjamin calls "sovereign" force.[13] Kracauer quotes a dialogue between two judges in Anatole France's *Les juges intègres*, in which one appeals to the inalienable nature of eternal law, whereas the other refers to how the law can be bent and molded to the particular age and considers it at best a natural product of social life, constantly changing with the latter. Kracauer writes: "If it was only the Law that were valid, then community would not exist, because the tension between the two positions would be broken too soon by the Law such as posits itself as unconditional. Were Law not to be valid, the community would have moved from the middle either upwards or downwards and would therefore also not exist."[14]

In other words, the human condition is by no means prestabilized by eternal laws, but instead the Law and what it signifies exist only in a tense relationship to each other; this tension first makes possible their existence somewhere between divine force and their interpretation and application of laws by humans. This position is the origin of the intractable paradoxes of notions of modern liberty and theological determination, Kracauer avers, since "the community's members face the paradoxical task of fulfilling within the median domain, as laid down by Law, those demands which humans make of one another. At the same time, people must apply these demands to the interpersonal domain, for the community must be adequate to the demands of life (which is shackled to the passage of time) and yet, in light of life's supra-temporal determination, must also eradicate these demands."[15]

In his reading of Benjamin's essay, Jacques Derrida returns to the paradoxical structure of the origins of force in theology—and this, interestingly enough, leads back to Kracauer's treatise. For Derrida does not remain content with an interpretation of Benjamin's text, but takes it as an occasion to reach conclusions that Benjamin might perhaps not have appreciated. Derrida refrains from some censorial tone of confining Law to the status of a sphere of pure power, writing: "Here we 'touch' without touching this extraordinary paradox: the inaccessible transcendence of the law before which and prior to which 'man' stands fast only appears infinitely transcendent and thus theological to the extent that, so near him, it depends only on him, on

19

the performative act by which he institutes it."[16] The metaphysics of the detective novel is based on a similar construction of Law and justice—that is to say, on their complicated position within the "spheres." The "interim state" that Kracauer has to evolve is given a revolutionary thrust in Benjamin's essay, as it generates the "revolutionary" force as the "highest manifestation of unalloyed violence by man."[17] The transgression of valid law—if admittedly not in order to write future law—is one of the themes that Kracauer brings to bear to interpret the chains of motifs used by the detective novel.

Benjamin has his eye on that revolutionary moment in which applicable law is overthrown and new law has not yet been established, the moment of "pure force" when the sovereignty of law-making and the destruction of law coincide. Kracauer, by contrast, is interested in that moment of shrouding when the precarious intermediate position is overlooked out of blindness. At the level described in the detective novel, the revolutionary sovereignty Benjamin evoked is reduced to a farce: the usurpation of the cliff's edge by the lemmings à la Raskolnikov. Kracauer does not give this interpretation greater clarity other than to state in the regretful tone of cultural criticism that the unconditional nature of divine law has degenerated into petty bourgeois conventions. These customs are then accepted as rules without those who obey them showing any interest in their contents, let alone recognizing them as such. It is at this juncture that the criminals and the detectives take the stage: the executive and governing forces. What in Benjamin's essay only divine law was able tragically to achieve in the judgment it passes at the moment when destruction and new definition collide is presented as farce in the detective novel. And what in Derrida's outline remains an insurmountable paradox and ironically tragic is something Kracauer identifies as "suspense"— the tension created by the way in which the disparate parts relate to one another. No longer held together by some transcendent quality, the individuals run idle and disintegrate into "molecules in an unlimited spatial desert." However, Kracauer knows full well that after the fall of religion there is no simple way back, no straightforward volte-face. Instead, the higher sphere plummets through empty space to splatter on the mezzanine level of mortality. He writes: "Into the empty space, filled with the confusion of concessionary tracks, the higher secret falls—mingling, no longer recognizable, with atomized danger."[18]

Kracauer thus brings Kierkegaard's doctrine of the spheres to its knees by linking it back to earthly existence—and he does so without resorting to the trope used in existential philosophy, namely the intrinsic reference to the self as the measure of all things. Instead, what we see here is an intimation of that notion of Jewish theology according to which the transposition in perspective caused by "disfigurement" must be made good in the sense that the bend in a spoon seen in a glass of water can be mended not by touching the spoon, but simply by waiting for the water to flow away. Thus, the "paradox of human existence" remains "concealed even if it persists unconsciously." The "middle," the space of human existence, expands to form the surface, which spreads like a second skin out across the "inside" and "outside," or the "higher" and "lower," thus forcing the two to coexist on one plane or level. Here, on this canvas, the description is based on "punctuating":

> Punctuating everywhere you look: here, the legal structure of action, there theft, murder, and other clearly defined occurrences that are devoid of being. The two groups confront each other, unconnected, and nothing tells of their antinomic relation, something which reveals itself only in suspense. . . . What is called for is their spatial omnipresence, because in their case external appearance takes the place of lost interiority. Sin (a destiny of being in the higher sphere), danger (which symbolically threatens from outside), mysteries (which intervene from above)—all these things that burst the temporary security asunder are uniformly represented in the lower regions by embodiments of the illegal.[19]

With his elaboration of the "existential paradox" in the first section of the *Der Detektiv-Roman*, Kracauer creates the basis for the remaining sections. It is not by chance that they are arranged according to venues and actors. The detective "wanders in the empty lobby between the figures, fully the relaxed agent of *Ratio*,"[20] preferentially in "The Hotel Lobby." He is the representative of a governing principle, of a higher reason, the only figure to resemble a god. It is he who can make the connections that remain hidden to the others. Irrespective of whether he is a German, English, American, or French detective, he is characterized by an underlying ascetic stance—like a priest or monk. In fact, he is on occasion a hybrid. The detective is dispassionate and incorruptible in his task of recreating the relational course of things and is the only person capable of reading the hidden plan underlying the world from the tracks other have left behind them. It is his belief that the world is rationally purposive in structure, and in the pursuit of this belief he devises a plan of salvation against crime.

In Kracauer's interpretation, the detective is one of the figures who are typical of Modernity to the extent that the detective's aesthetic form derives from the existential dilemma that irrationalism "still shares the one-dimensionality of rationalism."[21] For this reason, the psychological traits with which the modern detectives are outfitted are merely alibis for greater losses. The insight into the overall plan— by virtue of which the detective is a godlike Creator—remains merely a "pseudo-Logos." The psychological features with which the detective is invested, furnishing him with a biographical secret as the motive for his solitary existence, are, at best, an excuse.

While the detective is thus the bisected Creator who knows the mystery behind everything (a mystery that is soon unraveled), the police take the place of a legality devoid of meaning—legality that has left the higher sphere of law behind it, if only because it already considers the "absence of the illegal" to constitute legality. In the chapter devoted specially to them, Kracauer regards the police as social agents, the builders of a new form of public sphere whose task is to defend this space. He writes:

> The sphere [of this public] in the streets, hotels, and halls is not based on some mystery, is not the outside round a concealed inside. Instead, if the Ratio drives out the inside, the public (as the calculable, the abstract, the generally tangible) takes the place of any persons related to the mystery, a relation that created a common ground and which is certainly not characterized by the public sphere of a community. . . . The police has the task of ensuring that this public life, which is still not yet something, proceeds calmly, safely and in an orderly fashion.[22]

Readers expecting to find analyses of the material used in a specific literary genre in Kracauer's philosophical treatise on the detective novel will be disappointed. Although the study is couched in the tone

of the cultural criticism of the time, the subject matter that it addresses in order typically to arrive at a diagnosis of society remains
curiously vapid and indefinite. Interestingly enough, the entire study
contains hardly a single quotation or longer descriptive passage taken
from detective novels themselves. What we said about the absent
sociological contents of the study *Soziologie als Wissenschaft* is true of
Kracauer's *Detektiv-Roman*, namely that the approach remains entrenched in the categories of a programmatic system rather than ven-
turing out into the oft-cited "reality." Thus, the discussion of the public sphere to be protected by the police remains rather vague, without
Kracauer's attempting to shed empirical light on the constitution of
the "public" as a category. On the one hand, his approach endeavors
to establish the track to be taken by a critical interpretation of a specific genre that wishes to not be metaphysical. On the other, it remains decidedly ensnared in a metaphysical mode or rather in the
religious-theological legacy of such metaphysics. It is impossible to
guess whether he rejects the oblique metaphysical sidetracks of the
zeitgeist owing to the lack of a "higher sphere" innate to them or
whether he is bemoaning the fact that he is compelled to admit that
there is a metaphysical strand even in one-dimensional rational
thought. Such a wish for clarity is pointless given his love of paradoxes, but his decision to love paradoxes may itself be bought at the
price of that notorious myopia generally associated with love.

In the first two chapters of the study—*Wandlungen* (Transformations) and *Prozess* (Trials)—Kracauer is clearer in his differentiation
of those aesthetic configurations in which the detective as an artistic
trope is distinguished from other administrators of philosophical concepts. The detective in his role as representative of a rationality
higher than merely the legality championed by the police (a rationality that no longer has to justify itself) is an ironist. Kracauer writes:
"The stylistic device by means of which the detective expresses his
sovereignty vis-à-vis the police is *irony*, which brings rationality to
bear against legal force."[23] For the detective is superior, not only because his knowledge of the mystery does not obey some external division into legal and illegal domains, but owing to his masterful transgression of the borders between the two, "a gesture of rationality
which, although at first shrouded, later emerges all the more clearly

23

and unequivocally."[24] In this description, Kracauer also outlines the internal interrelations and patterns of action that make the detective a representative of ethics, someone who does not hunt others down, but instead exposes and enlightens and therefore does not require the final trump card the police has up its sleeve: arrest. The detective can masterfully leave this to the cops. This is, incidentally, a pattern of action later to be perfected in film noir.

By dint of the fact that the detective can shift into the sphere of ethics—in the interacting roles played by himself, the criminal, and the police—he is specifically the character who alludes to the higher sphere, albeit without this sphere being mentioned by name. Toward the end of the treatise, Kracauer places the figure of the detective in his later chain of extraterritorial persons, who, thanks to their intermediate position, are privileged as regards knowledge—just as, in a literary constellation, one person can play many different roles. The detective is thus both witness and agent, indeed at times also the agent provocateur of situations that must remain opaque from the perspective of those involved in them. Only thanks to his shrouded proximity to the "supra-legal" does the detective have the sovereignty that allows him not to have to take sides, for all he needs is the discerning gaze.

In the detective novel, however, the mystery—as the cipher of an intended reconciliation that has not occurred—is revealed twice over. When, at the end, the one-dimensional rational denouement discloses the mystery, this reveals the wish for the Messiah to come, a wish that people want to ignore. For in the aesthetic domain, "kitsch reflects the distortion of the Messianic by such an appropriation if there is a conciliatory ending."[25] "While the Messianic does not occur in human reality or only intervenes in it,"[26] kitsch endeavors to bring about by force a reconciliation that does not exist. Kracauer avers:

> The rationality which reveals all is a mind which bemoans the lost feeling that, with the creation of an unquestionable intrinsic logic, the end also appears. The ending that is no ending, as it merely ends unreality, teases out a feeling that is unreal, and solutions that are none are brought to a conclusion in order by force to create the heaven—that does not exist on earth. Thus, kitsch betrays such thought as has been stripped of reality, thought that cloaks itself in the aura of the highest sphere.[27]

What emerges here is just how deep the divide is between Kracauer's thought and the happy ending involved in Ernst Bloch's "utopia of hope." Bloch endeavored to find a secular form for the theological figure of the inaccessibility of the Messiah's arrival. Kracauer prefers a paradoxical trope: it is always possible and yet completely inaccessible.

We can say of Kracauer's *Detektiv-Roman* that it presents the patterns of his ideology critique prior to his methodological and philosophical turn toward a materialistically construed concept of reality. What is interesting, though, is Kracauer's insistence in his "philosophical treatise" that he is going beyond the boundaries of precisely such philosophy. For Kracauer is convinced that philosophy, by always speaking of more than just itself, must always also talk of some of the phenomena of the real world. However, the real world has to be understood as a construct we have made, and as such cannot only be described but can also be criticized. The detective novel and Kracauer's *Detektiv-Roman* are identical in this respect—they are descriptions of a world. To this extent, the *Detektiv-Roman* already alludes to the transition that is then accomplished by the essays later published as *The Mass Ornament*. In them, Kracauer undertakes to analyze the visible world as a figure of thought.

Surface and Self-Representation: "The Mass Ornament" and *Die Angestellten*

"THE MASS ORNAMENT"

The concept of the mass as has been used since the end of the nine-teenth century, above all in cultural criticism,* can be quite straight-forwardly derived from its prior use: originally, mind and matter, the unformed and creation, were polar dyads related to each other ini-tially mythologically, and then scientifically. "Mass" possibly stems from the Hebrew "mazza," as in "matzoh" or unleavened bread, and entered Greek and Latin as the word denoting bread dough or lumps of dough. These origins are still to be sensed in the theological debate on the material nature of the bread used in ritual to symbolize transsubstantiation. In this manner, the word "massa" that entered that form of cultural history as was influenced by Christianity had a double meaning, spanned the unformed and the formed, and was thus redeemable. Since then, the divine spark that brought the lethargic mass to life, or at least set it in motion, has gradually been secularized. It can at best still be discerned as a demon or Antichrist in a seduced or obsessed people. However, it is also to be found in those creations that are branded the products of hubris, such as in the legends of the golem or the Frankenstein experiments, whereby dead matter is ani-mated or the dead enter matter. What we see here is the tension between scientific and mythical views of the world.

There is a wealth of evidence for the link between a physical defini-tion of inert mass (later steered by Adam Smith's "invisible hand") and cultural criticism's gut reaction to the "rabble," that fermenting and malleable dough, which the powers-that-be can only knead with dif-ficulty and that has to be curbed by the institutional forms of public order. This link also constitutes the basis for those attempts at mass psychology that lead in Freud's work to an inversion, whereby mass psychology and Ego analysis are two sides of the one coin.

In this regard, and given his use of the concept of the unconscious, Freud concurred with the approach taken in Le Bon's work. However, he distanced himself critically from the latter as follows: "Everything that he says to the detriment and depreciation of the manifestations of the group mind had already been said by others before him with equal distinctness and equal hostility, and has been repeated in unison by thinkers, statesmen and writers since the earliest periods of literature."[1] Freud went on to make a crucial distinction: "A number of very different structures have probably been merged under the term 'group' and may require to be distinguished. . . . The characteristics of revolutionary groups, and especially those of the great French Revolution, have unmistakably influenced these descriptions. The opposite opinions owe their origin to the consideration of those stable groups or associations in which mankind pass their lives, and which are embodied in the institutions of society."[2]

Freud's essay tends to be read as directly picking up the thread of Le Bon's work, which is something Freud himself was less clear on. Instead of placing his work under the sign of cultural criticism and opting for a knee-jerk rejection of the masses, Freud ends by raising unanswered questions. For example, he inquires what happens to the mass in the absence of a leader, how integration functions through identification, and what impact the "separation of Ego and Ego Ideal" has. In Freud's essay, written a few years before Kracauer's *Mass Ornament*, the mass is already perceived as a complex of libidinous members bound to one another by their points of identification. Freud essentially views the mass as a leaderless primeval horde that has succeeded in the course of several phases of identification in giving its hostile and narcissistic aspirations a civilized form.

Freud, himself by no means an uninhibited utopian, considers the modern mass to represent progress in the sense of Schopenhauer's "porcupines". In Schopenhauer's description, these animals are capable of learning: "A society of porcupines crowded themselves very close together one cold winter's day so as to profit by one another's warmth and to save themselves from being frozen to death. But soon they felt one another's quills, which induced them to separate again.

And now, when the need for warmth brought them nearer together again, the second evil arose once more. So that they were driven backwards and forwards from one trouble to the other, until they had discovered a mean distance at which they could most tolerably exist."[3]

Here, ambivalence as an inescapable side effect of personal emotional life defines a need for some sort of self-regulation by the mass. Only by forming a community can the porcupines survive the winter. Schopenhauer thus no longer construes the mass antagonistically, but rather posits it ontologically: we porcupines must form ourselves with the mass and in it. The mass is no longer malleable contents, but form.

The concepts Kracauer uses in his famous 1927 essay "The Mass Ornament" are of interest in this regard. For there he elaborates a notion that is more phenomenological and epistemological in orientation and reflects on itself in the locations of mass culture.

The Epistemological Method

The first of the six chapters of "The Mass Ornament" can be read as an epistemological agenda:

> The position that an epoch occupies in the historical process can be determined more strikingly from an analysis of its inconspicuous surface-level expressions than from that epoch's judgments about itself. These judgments are expressions of the tendencies of a particular era and do not therefore offer conclusive testimony about its overall constitution. The surface-level expressions, however, by virtue of their unconscious nature, provide unmediated access to the fundamental substance of the interpretation of these surface-level expressions. The fundamental substance of an epoch and its unheeded impulses illuminate each other reciprocally.[4]

Kracauer's notion of the surface level has meanwhile come to be regarded as *the* central theme in his thought. If we trace this concept in his oeuvre, it soon transpires that it is by no means used unequivocally. In the introductory context of "The Mass Ornament," the surface level is used as a conceptual image enabling Kracauer to address the issue of the masses. "Fundamental substance" and "surface-level expressions" shed light on each other. Moreover, the "surface-level expressions" provide "unmediated" access to the fundamental substance. This "unmediated" access is to be found in the unconscious. The unconscious contains the key to the consciousness a historical epoch can obtain of itself. The unconscious is the high road a society can take in order to understand itself; the surface level is the dream society dreams of itself and enables an interpretation of society. The dream thus illuminates the dreamer. The mass dreams in the form of its ornaments. The substantive contents of the dream constitute the social basis of the mass. This would be the oft-cited psychoanalytical interpretation of the above passage, which can then be considered to decipher hieroglyphs.[5]

Starting from the spatial construction that can plausibly be derived from Kracauer's architectonic thought, we can arrive at a different reading of the passage in question. For we could construe the surface-level expressions as ornaments to be hunted for at a particular position, namely at that location which can be grasped specifically by these very expressions. If we read the passage in terms of the "position" instead of the similarity of the "expressions" to language, then the surface itself appears as an *ideational image*.

In a 1926 review Kracauer wrote on Paul Oppenheim's book on scientific theory, *Die natürliche Ordnung der Wissenschaften: Grundgesetze der vergleichenden Wissenchaftslehre* ("The Natural Order of the Sciences: Fundamental Laws of a Comparative Doctrine of Science"), we find indicators of a view of the surface level that has to do with graphic schemas. The core of Kracauer's review is a new form of representation by means of which Oppenheim graphically presents the internal, logical reference of the sciences to one another:

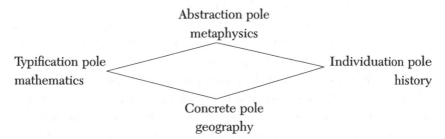

Abstraction pole
metaphysics

Typification pole   Individuation pole
mathematics   history

Concrete pole
geography

All sciences move between the twin poles of abstract thought and concrete fact as well as those of typification and individuation. The graphic surface between the poles takes the form of a rectangle if one connects up the four points of the poles. This rectangle "is the surface of thought and reflects in visual sense the two-dimensional rather than linear state of the logical order."[6] By means of this surface and then different directions, the sciences move toward the poles or away from them. In other words, what we see is a "graphic rendering of constant, *infinitesimal* transitions."

In the concluding paragraphs, Kracauer enthuses: "In the ideational surface, the spheres of Being recur that themselves cannot generate linear logic. The opposition of metaphysics and geography also strengthens the purity and faithfulness of this image. If metaphysics were to coincide with geography, then, as a heavenly topography, metaphysics would have managed to attain itself."[7]

In my reading of the connection between surface level and substance, I shall take up this image of an ideational surface: The surface-level expressions are intended to reveal information on history. The position of the latter is geographically defined in this surface, that is, pinpointed in the concrete form of mapping and details. The temporal element in the historical process can only be represented in this graphic, spatialized form. Its substance is the historical status as can be discerned as inscribed on maps. To the extent that Kracauer refers both ornament and foundation, both surface and substance, to each other, he fails to reflect the infinitesimal level at which the poles remain antagonistic in Oppenheim's model, endeavoring always to find correspondences instead of surface transitions.

Nevertheless, Kracauer's fascination with Oppenheim's model would indicate that he thought this way when viewing the aesthetic function of the surfaces, namely their purposelessness. The surfaces Kracauer describes have built-in points at which they tear, allowing us to see substance in them. Such substance emerges between the poles of abstract thought and concrete fact, and thus rationality and myth cancel each other out. Kracauer portrays this process by means of the movements and formations of the mass, which, as the ornament on the surface of society, he regards as the basis of the process. As a concept, mass is no longer separated from the ornaments in Kracauer's further thought. The mass observes itself in the mass ornament without being quite able to see through itself. The mass on the bleachers has a vantage point from which it can see the mass ornament on the playing field in the stadium, but it has no perspective on itself. The point from which the mass unfolds—namely that of the demiurgical director who nevertheless remains anonymous—dissolves. The leaderless mass cheers itself on.

Miriam Hansen rightly points out the following: "Kracauer's distress seems to be far less over the parallel between chorus line and assembly line, as is often claimed, than over the 'muteness' of the mass ornament, its lack of (self-) consciousness, as it were, its inability to read itself."[8] Kracauer himself wrote: "The regularity of their [bodies in bathing suits] patterns is cheered by the masses, themselves arranged by the stands in tier upon ordered tier." He continues: "Although the masses give rise to the ornament, they are not involved in thinking it through. As linear as it may be, there is no line that extends from the small sections of the mass to the entire figure. The ornament resembles *aerial photographs* of landscapes and cities in that it does not emerge out of the interior of the given conditions, but rather appears above them. . . . The more the coherence of the figure is relinquished in favor of mere linearity, the more distant it becomes from the immanent consciousness of those constituting it."[9]

To this extent, Kracauer's concept of the mass would appear not yet to have attained that level of differentiation reached by Freud a few years earlier. The two men nevertheless evidently concur when it comes to how the mass identifies with the ornament it constitutes before its own eyes. Here, Kracauer works at two levels, one structural, the other aesthetic.

The Structural Analogy—Split Personality

The structure of the mass ornament reflects that of the entire contemporary situation. Since the principle of the *capitalist production process* does not arise purely out of nature, it must destroy the natural organisms that it regards either as means or as resistance. Community and personality perish when what is demanded is calculability; it is only as a tiny piece of the mass that the individual can clamber up charts and can service machines without any friction. A system oblivious to differences in form leads on its own to the blurring of national characteristics and to the production of worker masses that can be employed equally well at any point on the globe.[10]

In this passage, Kracauer makes use of the common notion of capitalism as the rationalization of the particular in favor of universally available productivity which, unlike the laws of nature, obeys a rational logic. The production process rests on the paradigms of Taylorization, namely the division of labor to allow conveyor belt production; here, like the cogs in a machine, the human body is construed purely in terms of ergonomy and thus dissected, or, as Kracauer states in an analogous passage, is subdivided into "arms, thighs, and other segments."[11]

Kracauer goes on to say that the structure of the mass ornament exhibits a high degree of internal organization; it is a structure in which physical labor, psychological disposition, and the augmentation of efficiency are closely interwoven. On the one hand, he adumbrates that each "tiny piece of the mass" cannot be detached from the organized mass, but claims that the latter, in turn, cannot be separated from the formal, rational ornament it wears and constitutes. On the other, at this juncture Kracauer introduces the notion of a supra-ordinated "organization," without elaborating on this further: "Like the pattern in the stadium, the organization stands above the masses, a monstrous figure whose creator withdraws it from the eyes of its bearers, and barely even observes it himself."[12]

If we investigate the images contained in this sentence, then it will perhaps become clearer how Kracauer construes the mass in terms of the tropes of shrouding and visibility. The "pattern in the stadium" is the basic figure for the relation of particles of the mass to the mass: at a predefined position, the individual particle participates in a pattern that it itself cannot overview. For example, the fact that particle X at position Y of an ornament fulfills the function of representing the eye of Mao Ze Dong may be something that particle X knows if it were to know the overall plan including its own position therein. But even then it would not be able to see itself as part of the pattern once it has taken up its position in the ornament. However, Kracauer does not and cannot posit such a rational solution to the problem of participation and organization. The model of participatory self-organization by political masses in the symbolic ornament would therefore seem to be excluded from the outset. We could take political demonstrations in the form of candlelight processions, human chains, etc., to constitute such a form of self-organization. In this context, it would bear investigating more closely what shape the intrinsic link of formal ornament and political action takes or whether in fact aesthetic forms of protest are involved that are subject to a different yardstick. This is a problem to which I shall return below.

What Kracauer thus excludes is some additional ability to act, in other words that which Freud understood to distinguish the mass from the individual. For this reason, Freud believed the mass could act more morally than could the individual. Freud maintains that the formation of the mass can lay claim to being rational—as we have seen, this rationality first makes life sufferable for the porcupines because it fetters the narcissistic egocentrism of the individuals, constraining the degree to which each porcupine uses its elbows, as it were. In his concept of the mass, Kracauer cannot identify *this* surplus of rationality, the moral advance made by binding individuals together as a political mass. (Indeed, it was this surplus that Herbert Marcuse in his later writings, once more taking up Freud's theory of the libidinous trammeling of the individual to the process of civilization, endeavored to strengthen as a mainstay of a political philosophy.) In this regard, Kracauer remains entrenched in the concept of the mass as used by cultural criticism, a tradition to which commentators have usually understood Freud's essay "Mass Psychology and Ego Analysis" to belong.

What is interesting here is why Kracauer does not introduce the problem of self-representation or rather why he only addresses this as a negative quality when speaking of "illegibility" and "dumbness." The notion of "dumbness" can best be elucidated by consulting the exact wording of the passage. There, Kracauer states that the "organization" relates to the mass in the way it does to the ornament, namely the "pattern in the stadium." The "monstrous figure" is the organization, the "invisible hand"; indeed, Kracauer understands this here almost literally, for its "creator withdraws it from the eyes of its bearers, and barely even observes it himself." The "monstrous figure" is the overall image of the organized mass, and it has a "creator,"

33

which has shrouded the image of his creation. We can assume that the "capitalist production process" is the creator, is simultaneously cause and creator. This links the passage in question with the fourth section of *The Mass Ornament*. Following the proposition that fairy tales have a rational substance, which, unlike the older myths, is not believed and is grasped not as some explanatory origin, but as the pre-semblance of a different future in which justice can be truly posited, Kracauer turns here to the relation of humans, mass, nature, and reason.

The "*Ratio* of the capitalist economic system is not reason itself, but a murky reason."[13] Indeed, it is murky, because it "does not encompass man," and thus sets limits to its own rationality: "It [capitalism] rationalizes not too much but rather *too little*."

The rationally purposive is not yet that form of Reason that is anchored in the human being. Purposive rationality is simply self-perpetuation of the organizational structure and thus relapses into a quasi-natural state—and in so doing into mythology. This relapse into mythology is inscribed in the mass ornament. This is its obverse, whereby it considers the "monstrous figure" as a type of hidden Gnostic God and therefore Creator. Only for this reason does the mass celebrate the dumb ornament in cults. The ornament becomes the fetish that represents an internalized leader, the "monstrous figure" is the "rationale" the masses can "invoke."

Kracauer's use of the personalized image of a "figure" is not meant metaphorically but descriptively. It alludes to a hidden God, to the hypnotic Svengali Joe of the masses and is meant quite literally. Here, Kracauer's notion of the mass coincides with that of Freud, to the extent that it concurs with the latter's category of the mass as a descendant of the primeval horde: "What is thus awakened is the idea of an omnipotent and dangerous personality, towards whom only a passive-masochistic attitude is possible, to whom one's will has to be surrendered,—while to be alone with him, 'to look him in the face,' appears a hazardous enterprise."[14]

The "monstrous figure" is the natural growth of the historical process. The rationale underlying the latter has been braked and "is too weak. . . . Because this . . . flees from reason and takes refuge in the abstract, uncontrolled nature proliferates under the guise of rational expression and uses abstract signs to display itself."[15]

This is the predefined failure of the process of civilization, in which otherwise the primeval horde can become transformed into a civilized mass. Kracauer's critique of civilization hinges on the truncated rationality of capitalism and thus converges with the later thrust of Critical Theory, above all as outlined in Adorno and Horkheimer's *Dialectic of Enlightenment,* in which Enlightenment and myth become likewise entangled in each other.

To this extent, one could say that unlike traditional cultural criticism, Kracauer severs the Gordian knot of Modernity and does not allow it to disintegrate into two halves, but juxtaposes a higher concept of reason rather than some regression into irrationality to the rationality of capitalism. He therefore also makes use of a more complex concept of the mass.

Aesthetic Rationality

However, the more interesting strand of Kracauer's argumentation is perhaps to be found in a path that leads away from his critique of capitalism, ignores the reciprocal representation of structure and surface level, and focuses completely on the surface of aesthetics. Kracauer writes: "The mass ornament is the aesthetic reflex of the rationality to which the prevailing economic system aspires." Yet this is not all, for the aesthetics of the mass ornament also entail a more successful transfer of the "visible," which functions as legitimation for the mass ornament in the face of the obsolete forms of art. Kracauer continues: "No matter how low one gauges the value of the mass ornament, its degree of reality is still higher than that of artistic productions which cultivate outdated noble sentiments in obsolete forms— even if it means nothing more than that."[16]

The mass ornament unfolds its own aesthetic rationality not only at the level at which it adequately portrays reality, but also in its specific relationship to nature. To the extent that the mass ornament fosters the desubstantialization of nature, it fosters a more rational relationship to nature. For the real quality of the mass ornament is that it functions as a sign that does not falsely separate the body as a whole from organic life and instead makes the "segments" gel to form part of a "composition," emphasizing its abstract and artificial character. Kracauer writes: "Similarly, it is only remnants of the complex of man that enter into the mass ornament. They are selected and combined in the aesthetic medium according to a principle which represents form-bursting reason in a purer way than those other principles that preserve man as an organic unity."[17]

In other words, the mass encounters itself in the aesthetic rationality of the mass ornament in a manner unlike the merely reflexive position the mass adopts vis-à-vis the historical process of capitalist modernity. It relates to its body as nature permeated with reason— and therefore self-reflexively. Here, Kracauer's ideational images of the mass evidently contradict the conservative pole of cultural criticism, and we can detect here how he distances himself from some uncritical celebration of the mass and its ornaments as the organic form taken by the "popular body"—an approach to emerge not much later in the ornaments of Nazi aesthetics.

Retrospectively, Kracauer describes the switch from ornament into mythical rule ordained by nature when analyzing Fritz Lang's film *The Nibelungen*. The uniformly monumental character of that film arises from the strict compulsions of the ornament and Kracauer thus writes in *From Caligari to Hitler*: "The compulsion Fate exerts is aesthetically mirrored by the rigorous incorporation of all structural elements into a framework of lucid forms. . . . Certain quite specific human ornaments in the film denote as well the omnipotence of dictatorship."[18]

In these ornaments, the mass regresses finally to the status of a primeval horde that subjugates itself to the Fuehrer, whereby nature and the world are the screen onto which it projects its panic-laden images. It bears remembering that the historical caesura that juxtaposed regression to the intrinsic civilizing force of Modernity did indeed take place between the publication of "The Mass Ornament" and Kracauer's reductionistic conceptual thought in exile. Exile prompted him to study the history of the emergence of the German collective consciousness, and *From Caligari to Hitler* was intended precisely as such an investigation.

The debate whether or not Kracauer postulates a strong concept of the mass in Modernity as a counter to the regressive tendency, construing the mass as a body that could be unleashed at any moment, can probably only be decided by contrasting interpretations of texts written at different times and in different places. The ambivalence he shows toward Modernity as an epoch that has become entrenched at the level of rationalization is to be encountered as early as the first essay in "The Mass Ornament." Defining the vectors of the trends of the day—which Kracauer pinpointed by observing phenomena of mass culture in order to arrive at a diagnosis of his age—is something that is only conceivable because he uses a critical concept of Modernity.

DIE ANGESTELLTEN

Die Angestellten (Office workers) was the title of a series of pieces that were pre-published in *Frankfurter Zeitung* and then appeared as a book; with a wide range of different means, they all address the new phenomenon of "office workers." We must naturally bear in mind when reading these texts today that, as of the second decade of this century, various debates have taken place focusing on office workers, both in sociology and among social policymakers. The first debates were followed not only by the rise of trade unions for office workers, but also by a discussion among Marxist thinkers on the impact this grouping had on a theory of class. In Kracauer's work, by contrast, the essays in question consist of an astonishing combination of forms of literary and sociological description, including quotations from surveys and from interviews he himself conducted. Throughout, we can sense his wish for concrete empirical evidence that would as a form of description uncover the "construction of reality" better than would empirical matter. The incisive titles of the individual chapters abandon the sure ground of terminological designation and strict typology; instead, they make use of semantic associations—an approach already seen in Kracauer's clear preference in the *Detektiv-Roman* for a theory of names, a liking he shared with Benjamin (and Adorno). In stylistic terms, however, the short prose passages follow that form of essay writing that could be linked to the *contes moraux* of the French Enlightenment philosophers and to Horkheimer's *Dämmerung. Notizen in Deutschland*—published in 1934 under the pseudonym Heinrich Regius—not to mention Adorno's *Minima Moralia.* True to form, Kracauer introduced the chapters with an instructive two-part story:

> I.
> An office worker who had been given notice went before the labor court to file a suit for reemployment or for a severance payment. A departmental head has appeared to represent the company, a man who was previously the office worker's superior. In order to justify the dismissal he declared, among other things: "The office worker did not wish to be treated as a clerk, but as a lady."—As a private person, the departmental head is six years younger than the office worker.
> II.
> Accompanied by his girlfriend, an elegant gentleman, undoubtedly a high-ranking clothing manufacturer, enters the lobby of a cosmopolitan theater. It is immediately evident that the girlfriend's second job involves eight hours behind a shop counter. The wardrobe assistant turns to the girlfriend: "Does the honorable lady not wish to leave her coat?"[19]

These prefacing passages have a programmatic thrust. For, quite in contrast to the literary fashions of the Roaring Twenties and the Weimar Republic, Kracauer does not attempt to write *reportage*, but to provide a "mosaic"—and for Kracauer a mosaic is a careful composition, a deliberate construct. And only the latter allows us to tackle reality. Reportage corresponds to photography: "One hundred reports from a factory cannot be added together to create the reality of the factory, but remain for all eternity one hundred views of the factory."[20] While reportage "photographs life," a "mosaic" would be "the image" of life.[21]

In terms of methodology, in his mosaic describing office workers, Kracauer clearly also resorts to the figure of something simultaneously public and yet invisible in the manner first presented in "The Mass Ornament." The example he gives is the famous Edgar Allen Poe story in which the people curious to find the "purloined letter" only fail to discover it because it lies quite openly where one would first look for it were it not considered hidden, namely in the letter tray, and there no one would suspect it of being "stolen." Lying out in the open, the letter is only visible to the reader, before whose eyes the different perspectives and views are constructed. Like Jacques Lacan, who devoted an entire seminar series to this Poe story, (which Baudelaire translated into the French),[22] Kracauer also endeavors to construct the "reality" of clerical staff by means of various viewpoints, observations, and assumptions. He states: "Hundreds of thousands of office workers populate the streets of Berlin each day, and yet we know less about their lives than about those of primitive tribes whose customs the office workers watch with mouths agape at the movies."[23]

What is so fascinating about Kracauer's dense descriptions of the world in which the Berlin office workers lived and worked is not only the detailed observations he gives and the way he embeds these in a typological edifice. By virtue of his form of analytical description he succeeds above all in identifying a new characteristic of this milieu, pinpointing visibility as the projective surface for a form of judgment that itself merely wishes to assess whether it is viable as a surface phenomenon. The new visibility to which Kracauer alludes is something he outlines, taking the example of the "morally pink skin" an "incisive gentleman in the Personnel Department" regards as imperative during employment interviews:

> A morally pink skin—at one fell swoop this conceptual combination sheds light on the everyday world that is filled with window displays, office workers and illustrated magazines. Its morality is ostensibly painted pink, its pink is given a moral trim. . . . It would hardly be over-audacious to claim that in Berlin a type of office worker is emerging who is donning a uniform with a view to the desired skin color. Language, clothes, gestures and physiognomies growing ever more similar and the result of this process is precisely that pleasant look which can be reproduced comprehensively with the help of photographs.[24]

To Kracauer's mind, the office workers not only comprise a new type of worker, they also represent a form of capitalist rationality that had already become visible in the ornamental outlook of the masses. In this context, the sub-functions of the surface level are clearly also of a semantic nature; they mediate between the imperatives of the

"somberness of an unpainted morality" and a "pink which would otherwise start to blush in immoral colors." To the extent to which the
office workers suggest that there is a mean between the workers and
the self-employed, their external appearance is also intended to attest
to the reconciliation of the extremes enforced by the labor market.
The emphasis on visible appearances—including both clothing and
complexion, both "etiquette" and piano lessons—renders the office
workers even more transparent and would seem to introduce a seam-
less transition between the classes and social strata.

Kracauer finds that the transition in professions for women is a
typical example of this, such as their new employment as punch-card
operators at what were then the new Hollerith machines, long since
replaced by computers: "Preferentially, girls are placed in front of
these machines, among other things because of the fact that these
young girls have such dexterous fingers from birth; however, this natural talent is too widely spread to justify higher wages. When the
middle classes were still in a better state, some of the girls who now
punch holes nimbly practiced their *études* on their parents' piano."[25]

Kracauer refers to the close link between the cultural orientation of
the new middle class and the various forms in which high culture was
marketed when introducing the piano in the petty bourgeois living
room as a metaphorical ladder for social mobility: it led both upward
and downward. He thus points to the habit of intensifying the pace of
work by musical means: "A clever teacher cranks up the gramophone
and the girl pupils have to type away to its sounds. If it strikes up a
vivacious military march, then the typing marches onward. The turn-
over rate is slowly increased and the girls start to tap away at the
machines more swiftly, without really noticing the fact. In their years
of training they become fast typists, whereby music prompts the
cheaply rewarded miracle."[26]

Kracauer quite unmistakably adopts a stance indebted to cultural
criticism. Administration has been streamlined by technical means
and production planning is now based on the same, leading to the
emergence of semi-mechanical manufacturing—all this requires a
new type of worker. Kracauer's political critique is twofold. First, he
is skeptical of the office workers' illusory belief that they can distance
themselves from the workers and the latters' forms of organization

and institutions. Second, he is skeptical of the workers who, in turn, think they can distance themselves from the office workers because the latter do not grasp their role in the overall production process in society.

In this connection, Kracauer endeavors to make use of his subject matter to provide a diagnosis of society, an undertaking to be found in most discussions of the subject of office workers at that time. The office workers were seen as the harbingers of a significant change in society as a whole. Hans Speier wrote as follows in his major study of the social structure of office workers in the interwar period:

> The middle-class theory was, of course, hotly contested, but it and other positions all had the same effect: by focusing on white-collar workers, they tended to invalidate older sociological notions of society as a whole. Even if these notions did not always originate in a clearly defined, comprehensive conception of society, they all did assume the possibility of arriving at a general understanding of the structure of postwar German society.
>
> This generalizing assumption was shared by every theory focusing on white-collar workers, including Schumpeter's view that the increasing number of salaried employees would produce a bureaucratized future; the prediction of a brewing class struggle between white- and blue-collar workers; the thesis that the "mass character" of employees cannot determine their mentality and that the employees are entangled in an "artificial hierarchy"; Kracauer's critical contention that white-collar workers seek to escape from reality; and the assertion of the Deutschnationaler Handlungsgehilfen-Verband that the commercial employee is basically an entrepreneur.[27]

In his book, Kracauer traces almost down to the last detail the work and social world of the office workers. Yet Speier's characterization of Kracauer's study is accurate to the extent that it is applicable to that section of Kracauer's work where he endeavors to shed light on the links between the office workers' world and the realms of consumption and culture, in particular in his chapter "Shelter for the Homeless." Drawing on the insights afforded by a study by Otto Suhr commissioned by the trade union for office workers (and artists), namely the Allgemeiner Freier Angestellten Bund ("General Freelance

Workers Association"), Kracauer outlined the consumer behavior of office workers. The decisive difference between the office workers and wage laborers, he finds, is the different hierarchy in terms of the sphere of consumption: While wage laborers spend more money on food, lodging, heating, and clothing—that is, on basic needs—the office workers spend a disproportionate amount of money on culture. "The 'cultural needs' include not only health, means of transport, gifts, sponsorship, etc., but also tobacco wares, pubs, intellectual and social events."[28]

The office workers, distinguished from traditional wage laborers above all by their consumer behavior, become the champions of an ideology of the middle classes. In department stores, cheap clothing is dolled up in expensive decorations in the window displays, and products of different price categories are available in purportedly classless, reconciled simultaneity. The office workers' aspirations aim upward; and those who cannot drive a car can at least simulate driving and speed at amusement parks. The office workers try to make more of less, to create the semblance of the luxurious in the sparkling spotlights of the entertainment palaces.

In other words, whereas wage laborers attempt to mark off their domain in the public sphere from the middle classes, the office workers endeavor in a form of preemptive assimilation to approximate middle-class behavior as they would so dearly like to be considered members of that class. In other words, the office workers are not a stratum of society that locks itself off from the outside world, but they are upwardly oriented. And the new culture, whose patrons and propaganda agents the office workers are, is the culture of distraction, of entertainment, of consumption. The office workers are the better consumers, and the display windows of the large department stores are their Sunday school—there, before their very eyes whole ensembles of fictitious life stories unravel, biographies that serve as role models for them. It would at least appear as if the office workers wish to be classed as one of the better social strata. They quite unequivocally signal their will to climb socially in the aspirations symbolized by their trappings. They do their best to enter the ranks of the middle classes by means of mere semblance, by mimicry of the existing system of rule—something practiced day in and day out in the urban subcultures. There, burned out, they can enjoy the anaesthesia that helps them endure the anomie of their own life-worlds.

The example Kracauer continually returns to in his essays is Haus Vaterland in Berlin, an entertainment palace in which the culture of the office workers during the Weimar Republic thrived, as it did in the cinema palaces and department stores. Kracauer writes: "The visitors draw warmth from one another's proximity, consoling one another that there is no escape from the quantity. Being part of that quantity is facilitated by the grandiose surroundings. These are especially feudal in Haus Vaterland, the most perfect of its type, a type also more or less adhered to in the cinema palaces and *establishments* of the lower middle classes."[29]

The diagnosis of contemporary life Kracauer offers here is far more somber than one might think at first sight. Kracauer's analysis of the bizarre combinations of New Objectivity and sentimentality allows him to stress the motif of a life unlived that tries to evade its own barrenness by escaping into distraction. He puts his finger on this in what he sees as the Golgotha of the Pleasure Domes:

> The palaces exaggerate the style of New Objectivity, because only the ultra-modern is good enough for our masses. The secret behind New Objectivity could not reveal itself more forcefully than it does here, for from behind the pseudo-stringency of the architecture of such halls it is Grinzing which grins out at us. Only one step into the interior and you find yourself surrounded by the most opulent sentimentality. After all, that is the characteristic of New Objectivity per se, namely the fact that it is a facade which hides nothing, that it does not possess profundity but pretends to present it. Like the distortions of age, it stems from the horror of being confronted with death.[30]

Here, two strands in Kracauer's thought converge, two strands that are as symptomatic of his approach as they are mutually antagonistic. One motif is that of contemplative critique of the entertainment/distractions industry, such as Leo Lowenthal advanced in a key essay on the difference between Blaise Pascal's adage "that all human misfortune stems from one thing, namely the human inability to remain calmly in their chambers" and Montaigne's modern skepticism. For the latter diagnosed that precisely this need for nervous distraction is

43

the "condition humaine" of the modern age, "as variety always consoles, liberates and distracts." Thus, in the final instance the "borrowed emotions" will come to fill reality, "the advocate will be intimidated by the sound of his own voice and the gestures he has practiced and will be captivated by the passion that he himself presents."[31]

Kracauer takes up Pascal's contemplative critique in his critique of distraction. He identifies the escapist stance with the attempt to flee one's own transience and flee death—in other words, to avoid facing up to the thin thread on which we all hang in Creation. Indeed, he discerns Grinzing grinning in Haus Vaterland in the Baroque figure of "vanitas." But this is only one side to his thought. The other side, and here we could say he follows Montaigne, postulates that the surface is a serious playing field. This would seem to be suggested by his formulation "that it [New Objectivity] is a facade which hides nothing, that it does not possess profundity, but pretends to present it." As Kracauer learned when studying architecture, the facade does not stand alone, but stands in front of something or stands for something. Facades have a background from which they stand out, but which they can also represent.

In Haus Vaterland, New Objectivity is the facade linking the building to other forms of hotel and ballroom architecture, along with the decorations of the revue acts. Facades overtly blend with each other like fans behind which there is no face. The pretense succeeds in the final instance, but this is merely a side effect of the illuminations, which cause the fake images to shine forth in glittering stardust, something that can hardly stem from their kitsch themes. "Profundity" is replaced by floodlights that generate an aura, which ensures the deception works for a brief while. Kracauer notes in this context: "The real power of light is its presence. It makes the masses no longer notice their daily flesh. It clads them in a costume that transforms them. Its mysterious forces make substance of the glitter, make intoxication of the distraction. When the waiter turns the light off the eight-hour-day comes shining back in."[32]

One of the idiosyncrasies and peculiar qualities of Kracauer the critical essay-writer is that he manages to pinpoint such aesthetic elements of a poetry in the profane such as can then assist a trenchant ideology critique. Indeed, in the very moment in which we pause and become aware of the presence of things aesthetically, the unique fascination of mass culture shines through. It is no coincidence that the elements of the unreal shed new light on the facade and can transform it into a movie screen that imbues poetry with new life.

In his chapter "Shelter for the Homeless," Kracauer himself points to two essays that were later to crop up in "The Mass Ornament," namely "The Little Shop Girls Go to the Movies" and "Film 1928," both originally published in *Frankfurter Zeitung*. The fact that Kracauer himself locates the essays in the context of his study on the office workers is interesting, for it would appear to corroborate that his film criticism functioned as a diagnosis of his age. And yet precisely because Kracauer connects the new female consumer subcultures with the emergence of new professions for women, he has been subjected to a feminist correction. The feminist aspects are among the more interesting of recent attempts to update the reception of Kracauer's oeuvre. The essay "The Little Shop Girls Go to the Movies" provoked the question: "Why did Siegfried Kracauer go to the movies?"

Patrice Petro has carefully elaborated on the discrepancies in this essay, pointing out that Kracauer repeats the older equation of lowbrow culture and femininity to be found in traditional cultural criticism. This identification conflated women on the screen and female members of the audience. Nevertheless, in doing so Kracauer became one of the early theorists of the subjective and objective sides to film reception: "While Kracauer does not consider that women may have a different relationship to mastery and loss (and thus to melodramatic narrative and cinematic representation), his discussion of female spectatorship allows us to challenge the view of the cinema and perceptual response in Weimar as thoroughly streamlined, rationalized and distracted. In other words, even though Kracauer refers to female spectatorship and film melodrama in a disparaging manner, his analysis nonetheless suggests the existence of a mode of spectatorship and a form of representation that failed to keep pace with rationalized models in the realm of leisure."[33]

Other critical voices that have focused on gender representation in Kracauer's early essays on film, such as Sabine Hake in her article "Girls and Crisis," have referred, among other things, to the early study on cinema by Emilie Altenloh, *Soziologie des Kinos* (Sociology of cinema), dating from 1914.[34]

Altenloh, so Hake claims, had already used escapism as a conceptual tool in her investigation of the female segment of the movie-going audience, and in Altenloh's study proletarian women took that place the office workers occupy in Kracauer's essays. She employed *distraction* as her central concept, understanding it as a need and a form of social behavior to be attributed to social groups with no fixed roots in the social order, namely adolescents, women, outsiders in the urban world, and precisely that burgeoning group of office workers who cannot be clearly assigned a place in the binary structure of class theories. It is thus quite perspicacious of Kracauer to put his finger on the emergence of the office workers in the feminization of mass culture—particularly if we remember that the emergence of said strata can no longer be described in terms of the classical Promethean myths of masculinity as the productive sphere and femininity as the reproductive sphere.

An early critique of Kracauer's latent devaluation of female spectatorship is to be found in an article by Heide Schlüpmann, who writes: "In his reflections on the 'little shop girls,' Kracauer relapses behind the insights which Emilie Altenloh had already presented on the differing behavior of women compared with men, on their differing tastes."[35] In a later essay, she then distinguishes between the two essays "Cult of Distraction" and "The Little Shop Girls Go to the Movies": "It is in 'Cult of Distraction' and not in 'The Little Shop Girls Go to the Movies' that Kracauer takes the audience seriously as a productive force and develops elements of an aesthetics of reception through observations on the moving-picture palaces of Berlin."[36]

Kracauer's observations on the architects of the Berlin moving-picture palaces follow exactly the same game plan as his remarks on Haus Vaterland. The difference here is that lighting forms an invisible bridge between the elements in the gesamtkunstwerk of orchestra, spotlights, fabrics, and arrangements under the spots—that is to say, the bridge to the two-dimensional character of the screen. Kracauer observes: "Alongside the thoroughbred revues, performances such as this are the real attraction in Berlin today. Here, distraction becomes their culture. These shows are aimed at the *mass*."[37] What fascinates

Kracauer in the early essay of 1926 is the experience of something that is new in *aesthetic* terms and has to be kept at a distance by ideology critique. This also highlights another element that we shall return to in the discussion of Kracauer's writings on film theory, namely his obsession with the spatial image, with the construction of light and space in an event prior to the film proper. It is an aspect that reveals Kracauer's sensitivity as an architect, a man who is interested only in the second instance in film as montage—which is not to say that he was not aware of the quality of montage.

Autobiography and Social Biography:
Ginster, *Georg*, and Offenbach

Kracauer's two novels, *Ginster* and *Georg*, are among his most successful works. Although they clearly reveal autobiographical traits, we
cannot interpret them as romans à clefs. And like so many of Kracauer's works, the two novels have a complex publication history full
of obstacles and pitfalls. *Georg*, completed in 1934, was in fact not
published until 1973—as part of the Kracauer *Schriften* (Collected
Works). It definitely takes up where *Ginster* left off, the latter having
been published by S. Fischer and announced anonymously as "*Ginster*, written by himself." Both novels can be regarded as reflections
on Kracauer's own life and thought as an intellectual. Indeed, some
passages from the novels crop up again in his essays, although the
latter have nothing to do with the novels.

Hard on the heels of the two novels came Kracauer's study "Offenbach and the Paris of his Time," which he himself titled a "biography
of society." If we take all three books together, then we can see how
Kracauer construes the internal relationship between the individual
and society, and it becomes obvious that the strange vacillation between fiction and description is actually one of Kracauer's real
strengths. He takes the autobiographical, documentary material of his
own life as the starting point for the most concentrated observations
on the entire social milieu. By contrast, owing to the secondary material on which the book on Offenbach is based, there the descriptions
have the feel of fictionalized stereotypes. Together, these quite different forms of biographical narration paint an impressive picture of
Kracauer's obsessions.

The Offenbach study, which was in its day the butt of sharp criticism, can be read in this context in a new way. In other words, we
must first be prepared to suppress the suspicion that there is no element of biographical narration in it. And, above all, we must take the
title seriously; it informs us that we have in our hands not only a

monograph on Offenbach, but specifically a study of a particular city during a specific period. Seen from this perspective, the transition from the three books to Kracauer's retrospective diagnosis on the Weimar period written in New York, namely *From Caligari to Hitler*, comes less as a surprise.

GINSTER

In Kracauer's first novel, we can discern many of the motifs which—at the same time or later—he took as the subject matter of his essays and philosophical prose. However, quite apart from the motifs, in *Ginster* we encounter above all Kracauer's great talent for making observations and describing situations in such a way that the writing has an ironical twist to it. His idiosyncratic style, which lies like a heavy and grotesque linguistic sheen over the mundane character of events, gives this *key* autobiographical *novel* an alienating touch—making certain that we cannot simply read it as a roman à clef. In fact, we can easily identify many passages as expressions of what we could call Kracauer's photographic vision. This vision captures the surfaces—the language of surface guises is also the language that creates distance. And this distancing vision reifies, thereby highlighting Kracauer's own subjectivity.

Kracauer preferentially focuses his gaze on the proverbial outer guises people don—their clothes are canvasses onto which he projects their character. Take, for example, the passage: "The uncle's face was sunken, his skin not always clinging taut to the slowly sinking curves, but billowing out around some of the ruins like a night-gown, which, like a grotto, offers the body asylum in its hollow spaces."[1]

He takes a similar approach when describing the mother and aunt: "They walked off alongside each other, two hats, two coats. At first straight ahead, then turning right onto Main Street."[2] The distance created to the mother and aunt by means of the anonymity of the hats and coats serves to prevent any intimacy arising while still evoking the familiar, which can first emerge at a distance. However, Kracauer also applies the playful use of the outer guises to another end, namely to describe the experience of atomization in the mass. Following a lecture, for example, clothes line up in a row to take on sustenance. In short, Kracauer takes a visit to the restaurant and the time spent there as the occasion for a droll description in which the subjectivity of the people portrayed dissolves completely in the anonymity of the hollow forms and bodies, disappearing into their meals:

> He obediently followed between two coats, a constant process of short stops, continual obstacles; he would have been quicker alone. The gentleman who had known about the courts wore a fur. . . . Opposite the gentleman with the fur had previously sat, a long section of piping without a beginning or end stuck in a wing-collar. Whenever he got something caught in his throat, things were over for him. At his upper end he either had a bald head or pale, close-cropped hair. Ginster thought that a monocle would be in order. That self-same moment, the gentleman attached it to his eye, something Ginster regarded as a good omen. Paralyzed by having partaken with enjoyment of the wine, to which he was not used, he had to watch powerlessly how the outlines detached themselves from the figures and mingled opaquely. Perhaps he could blow through the pipe.[3]

Ginster's encounters of this type are not unique occurrences. Not only do furs and pipes seem to be aimed at him, even the ladies with their coats and hats do not make life easy for him. In this manner, Kracauer shifts the signification in a quite surreal way. He investigates the expressive and descriptive contents of such proverbial notions as the "lady in a coat" or "twin-set," the "flowery dress," etc., by shifting how these designations are used. Literally speaking, a "lady in a coat" can also mean that she is in a coat the way one is "at home" and therefore is invisible to the outside world. All those persons most active in the world around Ginster let him sense that he has not found an entry into "life." But with his innocent transpositions of meaning he is thus able to render them the passive objects instead of an animated item. Sentences such as the following are intended to create associative shifts like this: "She was a lady in a hat. Like a coastal cannon aimed to sea to defend the shore."[4] The lady is "in a hat"—as if in a harness; she not only wears an item of clothing, thanks to it she has also inexorably moved into a state for which textiles are the requisite mask. A woman entrenched in a hat, a man who is a pipe stuck in a wing collar that gives him a straight back and direction, worried relatives who retreat into their buttoned-up overcoats. And "the oval of the great aunt in her crinoline skirt hang from the wall."[5] Kracauer will return to this point later in his essay on photography, where he focuses on clothing, on crinoline, as a sign of the past, which photography would so like to be able to master.

As early as *Ginster*, the "oval of the great aunt" is placed in the context of a discourse on history, on those movements of history repeatedly given shape by the philosophy of history: at times, like the "uncle," they are "asserted in waves," at others "the aunt was more in favor of spirals."[6] Ginster is the skeptic; he distances himself from the dampened joy of his aunt's speculation that "if we lose the war, there will perhaps be a revolution here,"[7] saying: "It was not possible to grasp world history in the room, it simply flashed past the people without any physical form. Ginster was seized by a shudder at being abandoned; neither here under the light nor in its flash could he find himself. In-between: so much emptiness."[8]

It is not just such interpolated passages that have given *Ginster* the reputation of being a relatively typical book for the Weimar period. Like others, it was influenced by the experiences of World War One and the profound nationalist impact it had even among the circles of intellectuals disappointed by the fact that no revolution had been forthcoming. At the least at the time, the revolutionary seemed to be a heroic alternative to life as a soldier in the second decade of the century. Thus, *Ginster* would seem to be quite in keeping with its day.

Kracauer the author is quite critical in how he handles his literary likeness. In *Ginster*, for example, we encounter the details of that memorial to the soldiers Kracauer designed while a young architect in Frankfurt: "The competition was a public tender by the city, in honor of the dead soldiers and the suffering architects. A memorial cemetery. There were countless soldiers who had previously lived in the city and who had been prevented once and for all from returning to their homes. Their relatives wanted to have them back, and if not living, then at least as corpses. And the soldiers themselves would surely feel more at home in beautiful graves than outside them."[9]

This ironical stretto culminates in the complete instrumentalization of the dead, who take their place in the memorial cemetery for the good of the Fatherland and the unemployed architects, who, although never in a position to build apartments for the soldiers, can now at least provide their last resting place. Above all, to the benefit of the profession, *en gros et en détail*:

> The city would gladly have put off building the entire cemetery, had not a group of architects rebelled. They needed work as otherwise they would starve. Luckily, the population since the beginning of the war had grown into one community held together by fate. Given the lack of buildings required for the survivors, the city saw itself compelled to tender for the cemetery after all. . . . They were quite indifferent toward the object of the tender; they could just as happily have had tenement blocks designed. The plot of land bought by the city lay on higher ground, whence the graves had a marvelous view.[10]

Kracauer's novel on the young Ginster has little in common with the pacifistic novels that followed in the wake of World War One, despite its markedly ironic or even satirical traits such as those above, for they put the knife into the Wilhelminian era and the pillars of society at the time. The pacifistic novels tended to address the horrible experiences of the war, as well as topics such as death, maiming, and impoverishment with far greater directness. By contrast, *Ginster*'s perspective remains subjective: the war goes sailing past Ginster along with world history. The book neither takes to the "higher ground" whence the war brews up into a storm of steel, nor does it adopt the stance of the participant who is scarred by the horrors. *Ginster* describes the dead as so many graves. However, this ironic perspective is far more than just the deliberate creation of narrative distance in order to attain a vantage point from which to paint a portrait of society.

The quality of this novel stems precisely from the fact that the author also presents the central figure from a specific perspective. Ginster, scatterbrained, describes himself in terms of his dissimilarity to others and their experiences: "I have often brooded over. . . . how the others differ from myself. People are interested in their lives, they have their goals, wish to own property, perhaps achieve something. Everybody I know is a castle. I myself do not wish for anything. People will not understand me, but I would most like to simply dissipate.

That prevents people from getting closer to me. I sleep in an indifferent room and do not even possess a library."[11]

In other words, Ginster is the hero of the "in-between"; the absence of what he calls "life" does not lead him into the jaws of death desired with some pathos, but instead makes of him a modern construct of decentering. To this extent, *Ginster* is a truly modern novel, even if it is realistic in terms of narrative technique. Ginster, bereft of location, is a Kafkaesque younger brother of Robert Musil's "man without qualities." He is certainly filled with an awareness that there is no homely place in the "in-between" realm, that the anonymity of the streets in the metropolis is the only place where someone can tarry who is "dissipating."

The knowledge of our ineluctable contingency determines modern subjectivity which, even given the experience of death in World War One, desists from flights of historico-philosophical fancy into misery. Only the material world of objects affords eyes and language a brace with which to hold themselves steady.

Eckhardt Köhn has rightly observed with reference to Kracauer's early writings that they essentially devise "an aesthetics based in existentialism."[12] Köhn believes this can be seen as early as the essay *Die Künstler in dieser Zeit* (The artist in our time) published in 1925, where Kracauer postulates the aesthetic depiction of likeness as a figure of salvation. It is, needless to say, not easy to posit a meaningful use for the term "representation" with reference to language. For what is evident in photographical and photomechanical reproduction is not straightforward in language. Kracauer's idiosyncratic theory of language becomes somewhat more plausible if related to his own literary output—it is intended as a variant on the use of aesthetic language. Words do not depict objects; instead words evoke a certain perception of things, they are the perspectives on things. As a point of fact, the three-dimensional quality of the images in Kracauer's prose would appear to stem from such a use of language. The words offer us perspectives on objects. The word "coat" is a perspective on the mother who is thereby evoked by the image.

These observations may appear idiosyncratic, but they are intended to prevent readers from making the mistaken assumption that Kracauer's prose is based on some customary use of metaphors. The mother is by no means like a coat, the woman is by no means like a hat, nor the man like a pipe. No, this coat *is* the mother—first she was here and now she is that coat back there—the mother is in the coat—it is her form, her image, her guise, and definitely not some metaphor paraphrasing her.

However, Kracauer's use of language is metaphorical in the sense in which Martin Seel has defined a perspective offered within the metaphor, something that perhaps approximates best the images metaphors entail. Seel writes: "A metaphorical assertion does not assert what the sentence containing it literally says; it activates and organizes an illuminating and stimulating *reference* to the object of which it speaks. . . . What metaphor offers us is the chance to adopt its perspective."[13] We need to bear this distinction in mind if we wish to follow the "abysmally profound realist"[14] in his literary approach. Precisely this understanding of metaphor enables us to analyze Kracauer's linguistic worlds.

The refusal to adopt paraphrasing metaphors corresponds to the idea of a materialization of bodies into things that can be saved by representation. Needless to say, it would be petty not to admit that Kracauer's use of language has a metaphorical core. However, the metaphorical references are not to be found at the comparative level of components of things in the sense that there is an analogous relation between "mother" and "coat." Kracauer's aesthetic transformation of the customary use of metaphors takes a different approach.

Here, the coat offers us a perspective of the mother. We should not take the meaning of the words literally, but instead should concentrate on the images the perspective affords. If the coat is a perspective on the mother, then it forms that final point in a fictitious central perspective focusing on the mother and creating distance to her. The coat functions *as* the perspective in the sense that we feel we are looking through the wrong end of a telescope, distancing the mother instead of making the reader feel closer to her. The coat is a metaphor for the distance between the observer and the object observed—and not for the mother herself. To the extent that Kracauer prefers metaphors as perspectives of distanciation, we could regard his literary efforts as ways of creating linguistic space, in which a world of things is created *in* language. The things can be construed both as real objects and as those perceived by a specific subjectivity. To my mind, what is special about Kracauer's prose is this interweaving of different types of perspective: words can function as points of spatial perspective or, by dint of the images they contain, be used to constitute interpretative perspectives, such as the gentleman who appears in the pipe: he becomes above all stiff and hollow in the image of the pipe.

However, with respect to Kracauer's literary language I find more interesting those metaphors which, as in the example of the mother and the coat, attest less to caricature and more to a generalizing view of the world. In *Ginster* it proves possible through language to articulate this "dissipation" of objects (and this is the perspective the narrative figure Ginster has on the world) and to evoke it by aesthetic means. It is this which forms the basis of the specific aesthetic coherency in Kracauer's novels. The incredible three-dimensional quality of Kracauer's idiom is primarily an upshot of the images of his language, but it also goes beyond this and stems from a spatial perspective which, at the same time, involves derealization through fictionalization:

> The wide-open avenues of the illuminated bodies hung in its [the little shop's] mirrors—they stretched to the furthest vanishing point and with them, the ornamental shrubbery of bottles and little bottles became smaller. They formed countless niches which opened out onto the avenues. "Hair cut?" Ginster simply nodded, he wished to remain in the hot artificial landscape as long as possible; it constantly offered new vistas and insights. He was just contemplating a label whose ornate writing itself smelled good when he was torn away by the comment of a barber's assistant that more frequent cutting strengthened one's hair. "Please, only once!" Ginster replied, who believed it to be impractical to allow one's hair to become too strong. They should rather become thin like he himself. But before he could turn back to the labels he was showered by a cloud of perfume. The landscape lay undistorted in a shimmering flood of illumination. His own head was the only puddle. New visitors appeared, there was no space in the little shop. Outside it was cold. His only consolation was that he carried all the gossip away with him.[15]

In this longer passage from *Ginster* we can discern those interlocking perspectives that, on the one hand, confront the "abysmally profound" realist with that phenomenological gaze with which the scenarios of the barbershop can be described, and, on the other, juxtapose him to a form of modern subjectivity which knows that "reality is a construct," as one of Kracauer's oft-cited adages would have it. The strange relation to the world of things and objectified experiences is neither made to disappear nor out-trumped by virtue of being given a literary thrust. As if caught in the barbershop mirror, in language, the world opens out onto a different world in which everything remains in place and yet appears in a different light and a different perspective. The utopian transformations Ginster accomplishes in front of the mirror are not those of another world—they are based on things and only thus can they be depicted and be redeemed in images. The short description of how the confined barbershop widens outward into an avenue thanks to the perspective projected in the mirror already preempts Kracauer's later film theory. There, he insists that redemption is only possible in the representation of likeness, for the latter evokes that glimmer which can then condense to become the aura of the likeness.

The cuts made to the postwar Kracauer edition brought out by Suhrkamp in 1963 are just one of the many unfortunate stories surrounding Kracauer's *Ginster*. In his postscript to the edition of *Ginster* included in the *Schriften*, Karsten Witte points out that it was Kracauer's express wish that the final chapter be left out. By contrast, the journal *Marbacher Magazin* reports that editors and friends who were also Suhrkamp authors persuaded Kracauer to forgo inclusion of the final chapter.

Irrespective of the exact form the editorial decisions took, it is safe to say that when the book first appeared, the concluding chapter was regarded as out of place and was the focus of criticism. In the chapter in question, we can sense Kracauer's proximity to Sartre, something otherwise hardly ever mentioned—after all, the French existentialists and the Frankfurt School are usually considered incompatible. Nevertheless, parallels are obvious, probably stemming from the joint belief in facticity, on the one hand, and the reality of the imaginary on the other, not to mention both men's affinities to phenomenology. In this ultimate chapter we find the admixture of intensified perception as the sensualist inheritance taken on from materialism and a sense of existential determinism; it is a mixture which therefore all the more radically spawns a notion of freedom. It is a combination imbued with a coda of its own, as it were, with Ginster's move to Marseilles, and this breaks the framework of the prior chapter.

The end in Marseilles returns to the beginning of the novel, the description of a city, of urban streets and cafés. The Great War (the novel opens with the sentence: "When the war broke out, Ginster, a young man of twenty-five, was in the state's capital") creates order and a cessation of movement and thus transposes death into the distant memorial cemeteries. Marseilles, by contrast, becomes a mythical place of unordered multiplicity where life and death exist alongside each other. "There are now five years between us and the War," so the Marseilles chapter specifies, and Ginster now experiences time differently, experiences the moment when the complete dissolution of identity constitutes something new: "On the quayside, on the other hand, I was in a distant place to which no ship sails. A man was bidding a woman farewell, and she did not even cry—he was no longer at home, he was not yet en route, he was unattainably far away. Torn out of context for a moment at least, as if he were new. I did not really watch him, in fact I did not really watch anything, but instead slipped out myself, as if I were departing. It is only a matter of a moment, in which a minute hole emerges."[16]

This is Kracauer returning to that idea of sovereignty he had made his own in the *Detektiv-Roman*, with the difference that here it is the utopia of the empty moment in which the new enters the world. It is no coincidence that this conception of the new goes hand in hand with loss of memory and with remembrance being abandoned: "For him, it was too hot for the past. He had also lost his memory."[17] In the disorder of the Mediterranean port, life returns as an empty new beginning, but it is one bereft of memory.

We can interpret this conclusion in two different ways. It could be Dionysian in the Nietzschean sense of the loss of guilt through the abandonment of remembrance—here, life itself becomes reinstated as the sensual way of experiencing the world. Or we could read it with Benjamin's eyes as the empty moment of sovereign Creation, the

57

new as the moment of emptiness that is defined by the paradox of "nothing-left" although "nothing-has-yet-gone." A third interpretation would be to construe the fall into emptiness as the precondition for self-creation in the existentialist vision. All three interpretations probably do not fit the attempt to locate Kracauer's novel in a more narrow model of sociocritical discourse.

It is interesting to note here that the early reviewers were obviously aware that *Ginster* was not a realistic novel, but had borrowed much from the slapstick comedies of the silent movies of the day—in fact, that long passages in it are meant as comedy. I have tried to show that some of *Ginster*'s literary quality derives from the fact that Kracauer prefers a spatial perspective, for here distanciation allows things to flip over into the grotesque: "Ginster at war, that is: Chaplin in the department store. On the escalator which serves to move everyone else forward Chaplin stumbles 16 times. While all the others are shopping, he is pursued by Rayon's boss. While all the others pay duly and submissively, he is suspected of being a thief. Compared with the department stores, the wars, the tailors, and the mother countries Chaplin is just as helpless and cowardly as Ginster, just as strange and clumsy, ridiculous and tragicomic. We at long last have a literary Chaplin. He's called 'Ginster'."[18] In this review, which appeared anonymously in *Frankfurter Zeitung*, Joseph Roth emphasized the element of the grotesque in the novel. However, the comparison with Chaplin may be slightly exaggerated, as Ginster lacks all those signs of courage in the face of normal adversity and the wish to stick up for those weaker than he with which Chaplin's figure braves daily life. Nevertheless, the difference between *Ginster* and the pacifistic novels of the day is clearly evidenced by this grotesque trait.

It would also be interesting to analyze the novel by comparing it with the existential heroes in the novels of Ernst Jünger. We would probably find that Kracauer opts for a kind of negative existentialism. The element of the existentialist decision remains necessarily absent—neither redemption nor salvation are present as positive tropes. "I am going now, Ginster said to himself; tomorrow—he stumbled."[19] Inka Mülder-Bach rightly stresses the importance of "improvisation" in Kracauer's work ("I am in the final analysis an anarchist.") from which he derived a "dialectic of transient nature and projective freedom."[20]

The only positive frame Kracauer creates is the possibility of an empty moment of Messianic hope that the new could occur. However, it is a hope that can never be fulfilled in the novel. To this extent, the end, the concluding chapter in Marseilles, retracts the Dionysian intoxication of difference present in the beginning. For at the end, we find Ginster twiddling at the ring with which he sets a little bird in motion—not knowing whether it is real or artificial.

GEORG

Like *Ginster*, *Georg* also has autobiographical underpinnings. The material on which it is based stems from the interwar years, which Kracauer spent as a desk editor for the arts pages of *Frankfurter Zeitung*. "The novel," Kracauer writes on the "analysis of my novel," "is, in other words, both a social novel and a novel showing the development of an individual. As a social novel, it paints the picture of a society which begins to open after the shattering events of the War. . . . My book, as a novel of individual development, is expressly intended as a disillusioning novel."[21]

He started the novel in 1928 and finally completed it in exile in 1934, but it was not published during his lifetime, first appearing in 1973 as part of the *Schriften*. Although in terms of internal temporal construction *Georg* takes up where *Ginster* left off, this "novel of disillusionment" incorporates the experiences of the Third Reich and banishment. The injury Kracauer felt given the lack of solidarity his colleagues at *Frankfurter Zeitung* showed him when he was in exile is to be felt in the description of the internal power struggles and opportunistic goings-on at the paper. To this extent, the dimension of the "social novel" is instilled with a universalized sense of disillusionment. On August 25, 1933, the editors terminated all cooperation with Kracauer—under the dubious pretense that he was also publishing in the exile journal *Das Neue Tage-Buch*. In September, he returned to work on *Georg* and completed it at the end of 1934.

Although Kracauer had made quite a name for himself in France with *Ginster*, and *Georg* had already been announced by publishers, neither a French or German edition was then brought out. Thomas Mann, who had been asked to intervene to secure publication, wrote to Kracauer: "The high literary quality of your great portrait of society has impressed me, and the problem of the book, by which I mean its fate, occupy my mind on occasion. When reading it, I learned to value and revere its silken style, its keen intellect, the painful sharpness of its observations and I really must wish you that it soon be published."[22]

However, the "portrait of society" of which Thomas Mann speaks remains more artificial than was the case in *Ginster*. The portrayal of the group of figures who are followers of the wide variety of different currents during the interwar years, ranging from communism to anthroposophical thought, from Catholicism to nihilism, tends on occasion to dissolve into caricature. Given the various social milieus through which he passes, Georg is characterized by a process of decentering—at two levels. On the one hand, Georg takes the position of the doubting participant who can never quite take center stage in his own activities; on the other, the narrator observes Georg and comments on the action. The strength of *Georg* is perhaps not so much the depiction of currents of the day; however, it succeeds in interweaving subjective and objective experiences in a complex fashion.

A snail without a shell but with sensitive feelers, feeling and thus recognizing the world, describes a sense of retreat, the moment of pain when the somatic burns into consciousness. What is completely new in *Georg* is that here Kracauer portrays the somatic sensations of sexuality, of injured desire and rejected passions. Here, the metaphorical "in-between," the "transcendental homelessness" and the frequently evoked "exterritoriality" are anchored in corporeal experience, a level that otherwise remains concealed in Kracauer's work.

The novel portrays Georg's love of Fred, a boy fourteen years younger. Given that this love only occasionally experiences physical fulfillment, it may have reminded Thomas Mann of his own puritanical homosexuality that so went against his grain. In *Georg*, hardly ever is this homosexuality mentioned, even though it constitutes the basis of the novel.

Ginster describes the first instance of such love—the boy falls in love with one of his fellow pupils, which then gives him the role of an observer who writes about others with whom he cannot enter into contact: "At the time Ginster was in love with a freckled fellow pupil named Neuburger. . . . He forthwith compiled material on Neuburger in his little notebook with all the embarrassment of a hurt lover."[23] Later, he "would gladly have turned into a beautiful girl" given the "men gazing on" while he was subjected to his medical examination on army recruitment.[24] The irritations do not stop at his own body, but lead to a fragmentation of desires and perceptions—and these become manifest in *Georg* above all as ongoing uncertainty, of being attracted and repelled at once:

> "Look, Georg, I don't know what it is, I am still so young. . . . "
> "It's nothing."
> "I would like to spend my whole life with you, Georg."
> They kiss each other repeatedly. So strange with the close-shaved cheeks. They talk incessantly, talk serious and stupid talk, all mixed up.
> "I've got to go now," said Georg.[25]

This passage is set off from the framework in which it is narrated, for it is couched in the present tense. The scene is initially narrated in the past tense and then switches unnoticed into the present tense. The change in tense enables Kracauer to give the passage a directness that would hardly otherwise have been available to someone who "beneath the surface investigated the others."[26] In this way, the scene with Fred becomes one of those images in memory the continual presence of which *is* love and also pinpoints that moment on which all unfounded hope rests, that moment when the desired man speaks the magical words: "I would like to spend my whole life with you, Georg." The present first comes bursting in on the scene when the future is mentioned.

Here, the ambivalences toward the sexual, mistrust of one's physical desires, and the body's ability to seduce are shown toward both sexes in like measure. A fear of and wish for symbiosis hold each other in balance, in an intolerable tension that can only be lessened by turning one's back on it: "Fred's hips stretched before Georg and he glued his gaze on the slender boy's shape, on the swelling that

61

stimulated him. Like falling asleep, he thought with a flash, one loves face to face and not only the hips. A hot hand stroked him and his own hand sensed its way blindly forward to feel, to grasp, but finally they ebbed, inhibited by shyness, falling back feverishly."[27]

It would certainly be wrong to think that Kracauer's descriptions of the erotic ambivalences of his two heroes Ginster and Georg form the key to his own sexuality. The authentic traits in the portrayal at best betray those osmotic points where perceptual sense and somatic sensation constitute subjectivity. The ambivalence we encounter as such a predominant phenomenon in Kracauer's writings is not genetically related to sexuality, and yet simultaneously refers to sexual conflicts.

This ambivalence can above all first be solved through fluid transgression. Just as Ginster turns himself into a girl under the gaze of the men, so, too, thanks to a costume, a girl transforms herself into a boy under Georg's gaze:

> In the middle of the room stood a costumed Beate and awaited admiration with arms wide open. She grew out of two red trouser legs in which she stuck as if in funnels, and over them she wore a black jacket from which a few, outsized buttons protruded violently, as red as the trousers and bursting outward as if they all said "yes." Had not Georg wanted to defend himself against the ostensibly false magic of the costume? He was no longer aware of it. What excited him most about the figure was, however, this: it represented a mixture of boy and girl, a mixture of indescribable sweetness. The boy was mainly represented by the buttons and the trousers, which, taken on their own, would have had a decidedly impertinent effect. However, this brashness was offset by the girlish fear that stemmed from the high throat. Indeed, whereas the masculine elements of the costume betrayed an express desire to attack, the costume's high-cut throat resembled a caring cave into which one could retreat in the face of dangerous attackers.[28]

It would be too simple to subject this clearly stated delight in a bisexual image hastily to a psychoanalytical interpretation—namely that the creation of fetishes in masquerade is the secret precondition of desire. The "indescribable sweetness" is certainly equally the result of being "de-realized" in Sartre's sense. In other words, the costume as fetish does not stand for the impossible female phallus, but instead the "sweetness" is the result of the situation being rendered unreal, something that is stimulating precisely because it involves the realm of the imaginary. It is thus hardly surprising that only two paragraphs later the author refers to the fact that the image frozen in the mirror is what makes Georg unable to touch the girl: "By virtue of the mirror in his eyes Beate had become a picture, a mirror image, paralyzing him."[29]

Kracauer presents the metamorphosis from "ur-image" into "mirror image" as the female perspective, as her narcissistic dissolution. However, he describes this with such fascination that we might jump to the conclusion that such an experience was not completely foreign to him. Indeed, the above-mentioned scene in the mirror in the barbershop in *Ginster* presents reality in the process of its being rendered unreal in a manner similar to the following scene from *Georg*:

> Truly, Beate had shifted the high narrow mirror into the brighter light and was devoting herself so zealously to contemplating her own person that she became completely unreal. It was as if all life that she contained had spent itself in her likeness and she herself had paled to the mirror image of the costumed phenomenon in the mirror. . . . Finally, the whole room dissolved into the mirror and although the girl, engrossed in herself, continued to shimmer, so unapproachable, the impression was nevertheless that she had meanwhile stepped out from the surface of the mirror and was unfolding in spatial freedom. She suddenly dissolved into nothing.[30]

What is fascinating about Kracauer's description is not only the complex indirect perspective taken by the observer, by means of which he causes the initial bisexuality to dissolve into female seduction. It is, above all, the breathtaking construction of a reality that involves completely rendering reality unreal and yet is more than a mere artificial *trompe l'oeil*. The mirror image that comes to life and that Kracauer captures here is nothing other than the theoretical mirror image in his later film theory. With the introduction of moving pictures, the transition to illusion arises. Here we have before us a surprising precursor of that psychoanalytical film theory that takes as its starting point Lacan's proposal of the mirror stage in ego development.

Ever since Romanticism and its motifs of the mysterious doppel-gänger, the motif of the mirror image that takes on a life of its own is nothing new. However, it is impressive how Kracauer addresses the problem as being one of sexual identity. The stress here is kept clearly within the bounds of the classic conventions of projecting narcissistic masquerades onto femininity. Yet the motif of bisexuality and of transvestitism is introduced in a manner that is somewhat astonishing given Kracauer's restraint otherwise.

We come across a reprise on the mirror scene in the further course of the story when Georg, rejected, meets the "costume" and is caught up in a highly erotic scene at a carnival party: "'Now I have you,' stammered Georg into the blue haze. He meant the costume. None other than the costume—that at least was utterly sure—had challenged him from the outset and endeavored to demean him. He was filled with blind hatred of it. Of course he meant Beate, who had shunned him, but Beate and the costume were one and the same. She was stuck in red trousers, she laughed at him from the arrogant buttons. But now the tables were turned and it was he who would laugh."[31]

The aggressive seizure of the "costume" not only amounts to the story of a "fetishist" but also allows us to draw some conclusions about the literary background to Kracauer's prose. The trope of the courtesan, which again plays a role in his book on Offenbach, and that of the prostitute coincide in the fetishization of clothing. The "costume" completely takes the place of the desired woman—in the above scene it is not Beate, but instead Mimi who is in the costume; Mimi is more a frivolous woman who flits back and forth between men and with whom Georg commits a sort of public adultery. The "costume" is, in other words, a cipher for the easily accessible "femme publique," for the prostitute, toward whom the aggressive elements in sexuality can be unambiguously directed—condensed here to a Nietzschean "hatred of the sexes for each other." Clothing has a key phenomeno-logical function in Kracauer's thought for in this regard it functions as a signet for the surface level and is also imbued with a metaphorical (in Kracauer's sense) significance as a symbol of that which can be bought, as an advertisement. Perhaps what we glimpse here is the influence of the Offenbach book, which Kracauer was working on at the same time as he was writing the novel. The description of female clothing, which was a central theme of the French Enlightenment, is the decisive agent of sexual desire in *Georg*, too.

> For the bourgeois writers and intellectuals, the appeal of the courtesans stemmed from the notion of their artificial glory, the unreal nature of their appearance and their impressive theatricality. . . . In other words, the attraction they exuded was based on their ability to transcend the undesired directness of the female in a game of enticing signs and changing costumes, all of them extravagant and expensive.[32]

We can link this to the ambivalent constructions of the sphere of cinema.[33] The latter is characterized by a strange admixture of public presentation, collective enjoyment, and private emotions and in this regard is not unlike a brothel. In this context, we should also emphasize the enormous significance accrued to the street as the urban space in which experience was anonymous—and thus the basis for intimacy. These influences become apparent not least given the importance attached to "Parisité" in Kracauer's cityscapes, and it is these we reencounter in the book on Offenbach.

"OFFENBACH AND THE PARIS OF HIS TIME"

When Kracauer sat down to write the Offenbach book he had just completed *Georg*. The volume on the composer Jacques Offenbach was conceived as an expressly popular biography of an entire epoch— Paris of the Second Empire—whereby Kracauer construed Offenbach as its grammalogue. He started writing in October 1934, and in April and May 1937, the German, English, and French editions of the book all appeared. However, the popular success he had so hoped for failed to materialize. Indeed, the reactions of his intellectual friends all bordered on the vehement; some were extremely concerned by the fact that Kracauer, who had no particularly inward feel for music, had written a book on a composer that lent almost no voice to the music. In fact, he had addressed music almost exclusively as the basis for the librettos and these did not even stem from Offenbach's own hand. It is not quite clear why Kracauer so distanced himself in his

"biography of society" from his method of "immanente Kritik," that is
to say "intrinsic critique" from a viewpoint within the object—an approach Adorno championed. It was, after all, a method that identified
the socially critical substance of a work within the latter's internal
workings and never construed the work in terms of some external
analogy between epoch and artist. Kracauer's choice of a different
strategy led Adorno in particular to reject the whole study in no uncertain terms.

However, the project cuts across various trends, which seemed to
suggest that it might bring Kracauer the financial success he so sorely
needed. There was the fashion for biographies, one Lowenthal traced
in an essay on the subject, a trend that had become quite striking with
Emil Ludwig's biographies. There was the epoch chosen (on which
two popular novels had just appeared). And then there were the un-
flagging paeans that Karl Kraus, who had died in 1926, had sung in
praise of the composer. But quite irrespective of which factors
prompted Kracauer to write the book, one thing is not unimportant:
the fact that he chose to write a biography (and not a monograph on
Offenbach's oeuvre) meant he preferred a type of text which can best
be compared with a novel. Although it rests on predefined facts, a
biography must necessarily include free and fictional sections if the
historical persons are to be imbued with literary life. In other words,
a biography is a text to which dates, feelings, furrowed brows, tears,
and proclamations of love must just as much be added as must the
facts of proven *rencontres* and intrigues. Kracauer himself said that so
soon after completing *Georg* he simply did not feel up to writing another novel, omitting to say that this was only half the truth. Although
he spent the first few months researching Offenbach in Parisian ar-
chives and in the secondary literature, the act of writing proper con-
stituted an act of narration. And it took him a lot longer than planned.
This evidently reflects not just the amount of spade work involved
and the contract work he had to undertake in between. Instead, it can
probably be attributed to the fact that part of the ambition involved
was the writing itself. Even the most vociferous critics of the book
were unanimously of the opinion that the final section had turned out
best—and this section is certainly the most fictional and the most

subjective of all. It is here that the spotlight falls more on the sufferings of Offenbach in old age than on the major political developments of the Second Empire. Lengthier passages of the Offenbach book can easily be read as autobiographical projections, or perhaps more as identifications. In like manner, Karl Kraus had identified with Offenbach in part by using the latter's operettas as the model for the reviews he wrote of his own epoch.

We should read Kracauer's "biography of society" in large part as evidence of how he came to grips with his own exile in Paris. And I do not understand this in a purely autobiographical sense. For in almost all of his texts Kracauer focused on the channels of communication by means of which subjectivity and facticity engage in a constant nervous process of dialogue. Let us assume that the biography of Offenbach to a great degree had to do with the descriptive explanation of what we could term the "mystery of genius" in subjectivity. In light of this assumption, it becomes less surprising that the book reads like a novel in which the experiences of a historical person take center stage, something that emerges most starkly given the weak musical analyses. What we see is Offenbach as an artist of his day—what we do not see is the composer Offenbach.

In this context, the relation between the composer and his environment, the society of the day, his public, and his patrons is of immense importance. In short, we could say that the biography of an artist endeavors as a genre "to explain the enigma of his oeuvre rationally from the standpoint of his surroundings." And, or so Ernst Kris and Otto Kurz continued in their 1934 study *Die Legende von Künstler* (The legend of the artist): "There seems to be a twofold link between biography writing and the course of the person's life. The biography outlines the typical occurrences, and the typical fate of a professional group is characterized by dint of the biography—a typical fate to which the active person has to submit somehow. This link pertains not exclusively or in particular to the conscious thought and action of the individual (such as would be represented by a particular 'professional ethos'), but is to be located in the domain of the unconscious. The psychological domain to which we are alluding here can be understood in terms of a 'lived vita'."[34] In this light, we could read

Kracauer's *Offenbach* as an attempt by means of biography to redeem precisely those motifs in which the artist's career reappears in the guise of how the culture of the day saw itself.

If we therefore ignore for a moment that accusatory debate about the absence of the musical analyses—a charge leveled above all by Adorno—which would have formed the indispensable tool of intrinsic critique, then we can read the Offenbach book from different perspectives, namely as both a novel about an artist and a novel about society. The extent to which Kracauer succeeds in interlocking the perspectives of these two themes or whether all that is achieved is a work of mere analogy or unrelated parallel lines shall remain a moot point. A third perspective he adopts is autobiographical: *Offenbach* as the continuation of *Ginster* and *Georg*. From this third perspective, we could expect to find pointers to how Kracauer saw himself as an artist, for example as regards the importance of comedy. In the case of an author who reflects on himself as greatly as did Kracauer, and in whose oeuvre parts of the novel clearly function in their entirety as essays and were even published as such, we can likewise easily presume that biographical narration will have soaked up autobiographical traits or incorporate experiences of Kracauer's own day.

At this juncture, we must leave it to the Offenbach experts to separate the biographical statements Kracauer takes onboard from previous biographies from those he makes based on his own archival research. I am less interested in the origins of the materials and more in the way it is expanded on in fiction—in the sense of trends in biographies and those patterns in biographies of artists which, irrespective of whether they stem from older biographies or have been evoked by Kracauer, then become part of the legend Kris believes is otherwise the product of anecdotes passed down in the course of time.

Kracauer above all uses the model of "genius as a feel for congruency," to put it ironically. He writes: "Just at that time he was making his first appearances, the Paris that was to adopt him as its own, the Paris of the Boulevards, was coming into being. His environment leaped to meet him, and he kindled his genius on it."[35] Yet, he does not shy from a more psychological presentation, something he underpins by applying the muscle of legendary contemporaries of the composer: "Not so Offenbach: He had to be in perpetual contact with the world about him in order to be creative at all. All who knew him bear witness to the fact that he was the very personification of sociability. He plunged into social life because it alone supplied him with the necessary tensions. He lived in the instant, reacting delicately to social change and constantly adapting himself to them."[36]

Kracauer's emphasis not only on Offenbach's Jewish origins but also on the operetta are one of the provocative ideas and indications of the stress on biography Kracauer championed. Benjamin referred expressly to this in his correspondence with Adorno on Kracauer's book. The correspondence is truly not lacking in sad competitive allures (in this respect the letters in question are not untypical of the tense situation of life as an exile), and Adorno mentioned that he was considering terminating his friendship with Kracauer on account of the Offenbach book. Benjamin wrote: "What I consider the real flaw in the book is its apologetic character. This is flagrantly obvious especially in the passages which refer to Offenbach's Jewish origins. Kracauer discerns this Jewishness only in Offenbach's origins. He does not for a moment think of pinpointing it in the music itself."[37]

Benjamin finds that Kracauer has reduced "redemptive critique" to mere apology in a particularly shrill manner precisely where the apology refers to the composer's Jewish origins. And Kracauer does indeed devote an entire chapter to this topic.

Superficially, the chapter in question deals with the history of *Rebecca*, a highly successful waltz in which Offenbach combined melodies from synagogue music with waltz rhythms. For precisely this reason, contemporaries took note of it and also criticized it. By drawing on a biographical anecdote, Kracauer attempts to interpret this amalgamation of synagogue and waltz as homesickness. This homesickness is not the product of having left the synagogue of his hometown of Cologne behind him, but instead refers to "the homeland designated by the prophets."[38] In a capsule description of the life of Offenbach's father, Kracauer emphasizes that Offenbach came into close contact with Jewish players who also performed in the synagogue and was therefore familiar at an early age with the possibilities of crossover compositions that brought together the sounds of the synagogue and those of secular life, merging entertainment and serious music. Here we encounter a sociohistorical thesis that involves more than reducing the waltz to a matter of Offenbach's origins. For Kracauer describes the links between the emergence of popular culture from the everyday worlds of religious and liturgical traditions and occasions, on the one hand, and the corresponding performances by traveling musicians, such as his father, who traveled from his hometown of Offenbach to Cologne, on the other: "When he left Offenbach at the age of twenty to see what the world had to offer him, he quickly blossomed into a wandering musician, going from synagogue to synagogue as cantor, in the usual fashion of Jewish musicians, and fiddling at all the taverns he passed on the way. In the course of his wanderings he came in 1802 to Deutz, a suburb and entertainment center of Cologne. Deutz was full of dance-halls, gambling-rooms, and inns, and several Jewish tavern bands were established there."[39]

Kracauer describes Offenbach's father as an "understanding" man committed to "the idea of emancipation," a man full of humor and musical talent who eventually found full-time employment as a cantor at the Cologne synagogue. It was he who helped his son embark on a musical career and it was he who helped Offenbach get to Paris, where the latter led the complex life of an "aerial" spirit. Kracauer draws on this as an explanation with which to characterize Offenbach as "Ariel":

In other words, the realm of gaiety he aimed for was neither purely fixed in the past nor in the future, for it was neither pinpointed in time nor in space. It was not for nothing that Offenbach used many familiar, traditional tunes in his compositions, tunes which, like fairy-tales, belong neither to any specific culture, nor to any specific age. The Jewish musicians of whom he had been told by his father wandered from place to place, playing traditional popular tunes to the greater glory of God. *Offenbach's gaiety was assigned to the no-where, which he swept into as easily as Ariel.*[40]

When Kracauer terms Offenbach "Ariel," he automatically already gives his interpretation strong roots. Indeed, there are more than just biographical origins at work here. For the term "Ariel" is also the name for Jerusalem and synonymous with a sacrificial altar.

The strange quality of timelessness and spacelessness characteristic of the "domain of cheer" is, after all, latent in the name "Ariel," that promise of a Jerusalem of salvation and justice: "Yea, it shall be at an instant suddenly. Thou shall be visited of the LORD of hosts with thunder, and with earthquake, and great noise, with storm and tempest, and the flame of devouring fire. And the multitude of all the nations that fight against Ariel, even all that fight against her and her munition, and that distress her, shall be as a dream of a night vision. It shall be as when an hungry *man* dreameth, and, behold, he eateth; but he awaketh, and his soul is empty" (Isaiah 29:6–8).

Such references show clearly how strongly Kracauer identified with Offenbach, the Ariel. It therefore seems all the more petty to read the identification with Offenbach's Jewishness as some cheap apology. By contrast, the critic in the *New York Review of Books* treated the topic far more sympathetically, stressing precisely this background as an interesting interpretative platform.[41]

From the very outset, the different editions of the book contained illustrations and at times it would seem as if Kracauer based his interpretations not just on the written material but also on the pictures. His visual imagination takes pride of place over his musical fantasy especially when presenting Offenbach's stage productions. The motifs he discovered in Offenbach he then traced back along the Ariadne's thread of his own life into the nineteenth century. He accordingly compared Offenbach's music with Chaplin's films, identified the emergence of newspapers as the platform that promoted the entertainment industry (he writes of the "newspaper and love industry"), and discerned in the "surface" that ambivalent structure which had fascinated him since the 1920s. In certain passages, he regards this structure as symbolic of the "superficiality" of fashions spawned by the media, whereas in others he reads it as the token of a form of mobility first generated by Offenbach's music:

> Some of his operettas are merely the equivalent of musical journalism.
>
> The facility with which he created reinforced his inclination to satisfy the great demand for his work in summary fashion. Saint-Saens observed that his score swarmed with microscopic little notes, like flies' feet, and out of sheer hurry barely touched the paper. There was a connection

71

between Offenbach's work—that is, on those occasions when it is evident—and the bond that tied him to the surface of life. A few phrases that he wrote at the age of fifty-five, looking back on his immense output and a whole lifetime of experience, illustrate how strongly he tended by nature to take into account the transitoriness, the impermanence of things.[42]

The subjective side to a literary identification is only one side to things—and in this regard Kracauer seemed quite content to abide by the hidden codes of biographies of artists and to create new variants of them. Thus, precisely the final chapter on Ariel's race to defy death by increasing the tempo of his work as a composer is a truly gripping portrayal.

However, our interpretation should not allow us to forget the second, discerning side to the work, namely the portrait of an epoch. Kracauer shared with Walter Benjamin an interest in nineteenth-century Paris. Benjamin's fragmentary *Passagen-Werk* goes the opposite way of Kracauer's narrative: while Kracauer turns all the source material into a novel, Benjamin presents all the source material without any text of his own. However, both men shared the view that the epoch in question was the most significant of melting pots and that in it the rudiments of twentieth-century streams of consciousness and phenomena were stirred up. The idea Benjamin and Kracauer pursue is that the epoch inscribed its signature in the surface of all the phenomena it spawned—and with Offenbach it is judged to have also written the music that caused its own conditions to dance.

Kracauer's endeavor might have turned out far more impressively if he had forgone his adherence to the biography of an artist as a red thread he had to follow. Let us compare *Offenbach*, for example, with Jean-Paul Sartre's *The Family Idiot. Gustave Flaubert*, which returns a few decades later to the same epoch which, to Kracauer's mind, was epitomized by the phenomenon of Offenbach and should be connected with his name.[43] Sartre, too, essays to interweave "subjective and objective" neurosis, to focus on the historical conditions in which, by virtue of reification, the autonomy of art eventually emerged. "I thought it permissible, for this difficult test case, to choose a compliant subject who yields himself easily and unconsciously."[44] This painful process is what Sartre dissects when studying the life and work of Gustave Flaubert. "A corpse," he writes, "is open to all comers."[45] The "individual universal" Sartre has in mind and which he imagines over several thousand pages is nothing other than what Kracauer's physiognomy of an epoch tries to describe in the traits of the biography of one individual person. It would be an exaggeration to say that Kracauer was completely successful. To a certain extent, the book is too undecided on too many aspects, the keen eye behind his novels blurs in the telescopic focus on the past, the reflective density of the essays is obscured in the concentration on the anecdotal. However, the book is strong on detail, and we can regard these as often full of daringly pioneering notions. His descriptions of the world expositions are a case in point.

We can perhaps pinpoint the oft-cited weaknesses of the book more precisely when comparing it with Sartre's opus. It does, indeed, exhibit a certain one-sidedness, which stems from the fact that Kracauer endeavors to reduce all the tensions of the age to one single pattern without seeing that at the same time antipodes arise in the radical autonomy art assumes. This reductive and one-sided view necessarily gives rise to contradictions. The epoch of Modernity is characterized by reification (the commodity becomes a fetish), alienation (the dissolution of a direct relationship to nature is the necessary precondition of modern subjectivity), and the emergence of science (humans and society become self-monitoring and self-calculating systems). Yet Kracauer's portrayal of the signs of this epoch in the upheavals of the Second Empire remains stuck halfway. In the dilemma between an outdated sham feudalism and the cold rationalizations of civil society, both Flaubert and Offenbach side with the Royalists, the former in the name of art, the latter in the name of modern entertainment. For both Kracauer and Offenbach, in the final analysis justice is only something found in fairy tales, whereas for Sartre and Flaubert the aesthetic is only to be found in the materiality of words rather than beyond them in the empirical world of the signified. The tension this creates (and from which the differences in the definition of what constitutes the "modern" arise) tears Sartre's book apart and is the basis for his "disturbed" relation to Flaubert. Kracauer's interest is quite different. We could say that he keeps telling the story at the point where Sartre or Flaubert break off, with the death of Emma Bovary who dies when facing the aesthetic yearning for feudal glory and the instrumental rationality of a provincial apothecary—under the helpless eyes of a paralyzed petty bourgeois man.

Bovary's daughter, who will go to work in a factory, is rather more part of the fictitious material for the literary productions of the boulevard in Kracauer's book. The small shop girls who cannot yet go to the cinema instead people the stage: "Nothing could be more simple than to drum together many of these girls from the factories, the fashion and tailor studios and the small furnished apartments. They were all happy to earn 20 to 30 sous an evening on the side, and when their naked flesh shone forth on the stage, no one noticed their proletarian background any longer. Flesh was universally human."[46]

Proletarianization turns representation on its head: disguised as commodities and as fetishes the masses now present themselves. Autonomous art goes into exile in the imagination—and this is also where *Offenbach* ends: "Had he not been a middleman between time and eternity he would scarcely have exercised the minds of posterity ever since."[47] as Kracauer tenderly says of his Ariel. When Offenbach dies, some "realized that day that the jester's work had been more serious than that of many whose seriousness was but a joke."[48]

Continuity and Mentality:
"From Caligari to Hitler"

ALONGSIDE Béla Balázs and Rudolf Arnheim, Kracauer was the third major film critic of the Weimar Republic to be forced into exile. We can quite unabashedly term him one of the founders of film theory, who, in his essays of the 1920s, had already foreseen with great perspicacity many of the later cultural developments traced in *The Mass Ornament*. In a manner that went well beyond what one would expect from a newspaper film critic in terms of aesthetic or other value judgments, Kracauer detected in individual films a new culture that arose with cinema. In this context, he was just as interested in the dominating architecture of the cinema houses as he was in the hierarchical structure of the dramatics and the stage sets of the films proper. Kracauer paid special attention to both areas, which unjustly earned him the reputation of someone more interested in a sociological analysis of the films' contents than in the aesthetic revaluation they sparked.

A lecture he held in 1932 before Berlin cinema owners and titled "Über die Aufgabe des Filmkritikers" (On the tasks of a film critic) has for far too long been regarded solely as a profession of his beliefs on the subject. The fact that an element of provocation may have been involved has gone unnoticed. Above all, his pronouncement that "a premier film critic . . . is only conceivable as a social critic" is what commentators have remembered and has been wrongly equated with the following: "His mission is: to uncover the social ideas and ideologies concealed in your average film and, by means of these revelations, to break the influence of the films themselves wherever necessary."[1] Even at the time, Kracauer knew that ideology critique could not simply be used as a political and practical instrument, and he was, of course, aware that a critic's pronouncements were hardly going to help precisely where it was necessary to break a film's spell. One of the first studies Kracauer composed in exile in New York was

Propaganda and the Nazi War Film and one of the questions to which he constantly returned throughout the 1940s was what influence propaganda and prejudices had specifically on the products of mass entertainment.

His own dramatic path to New York led him back to film as one of the focal points of his work, one he had never really abandoned. Not only had he written additional film reviews while in exile in Paris and jotted down notes for a theory of film, but the "bread-winning" work of the Offenbach book points out of the nineteenth century toward the institutions and phenomena of twentieth-century mass culture. By then, the murky alliance of cinema and politics—it advanced that "aestheticization of politics" in film-based propaganda Benjamin had viewed as the harbinger of doom in his essay on the mechanical repro-duction of the artwork—had long since become a reality and Kra-cauer concentrated precisely on these phenomena. With the stipend granted him by the Museum of Modern Art, Kracauer set out to write a history of German film. It was a history that had less to do with film history in the usual sense. Instead, he was interested in applying a diagnostic approach with which to filter from the filmic texts the stance underlying the actions of people on the historical stage. This ambitious project can therefore be seen as an attempt to reconstruct film history as a history of attitudes.

There are obvious difficulties in such a project—and little has changed in this respect in the years that have passed. Although *From Caligari to Hitler: A Psychological History of the German Film* has meanwhile become one of the best known of Kracauer's works, it is also one of the most controversial for reasons to be found at various levels. One is historical contingency, the others are of a methodologi-cal nature.

What were historically contingent were the conditions under which Kracauer worked. He hardly had access to copies of films; that is to say, he had to access forty years of film history from memory in such a manner that the memories met the minimum requirements for an intrinsic analysis. In New York to this very day people recount how he erected a veritable tower of books around himself in the library in order to better concentrate and seal himself off from other readers.[2] Within this paper tower he probably tried (working from his notes, descriptions, and reviews of the films) to bring the films so vividly to life in his mind that he could interpret them once more. The vagueness that resulted from these far-from-ideal circumstances is the key feature of the book; this annoys above all *film* historians, who would, however, change little as far as the study's methodology goes—if only it were not for that vagueness.

The methodological problems are of a quite different nature. In the last chapter of this book I will give an example of the differences between Kracauer's aesthetic appraisal of individual films and how he viewed them in terms of ideology critique; each interpretation is a matter of when he commented on them. However, this difference is not the product of an inexactness in his knowledge of film history owing to his having lacked an opportunity to check his facts; instead, it is a change in perspective that evidently results from a hermeneutic standpoint. Kracauer told the history of German film from the vantage point of its present end, and the present end was, in his case, the Third Reich. To this extent, he construed his book as a contribution "to the understanding of Hitler's ascent and ascendancy."[3]

In the brief introduction, Kracauer outlined his reasons for gearing the book to such a selection of issues. Primarily, he endeavored to tackle the thankless task of providing justifications for "mentality" as a historiographical category. This would be no mean achievement, as it has to be accomplished at two levels of the history he intended to write, namely at the level of film history and that of contemporary political history. Precisely the debates on the interconnections of contemporary political actions and collective memory, as were being conducted at the time in the wake of Maurice Halbwachs's pioneering study, show how up-to-date Kracauer's approach to psychohistory was.

Kracauer proceeded from the assumption that "behind the overt history of economic shifts, social exigencies and political machinations runs a secret history involving the inner dispositions of the German people."[4] And these, he believed, lay encoded in the films. Only these dispositions "explain the tremendous impact of Hitlerism and the chronic inertia in the opposite camp."[5] In this context, Kracauer drew support from his own *Die Angestellten*. He suggested that the Nazis' rise to power could only be grasped against the background of the weak roots democratic ideals had put down in the consciousness of broad sections of the population. To his mind, this was a psychological problem and he tried to support his hypothesis by referring to Franz Neumann's book on the Third Reich, *Behemoth*, and to a study by Erich Fromm (which was to play a decisive role in Kracauer's theory of the different "social characters"), not to mention Horkheimer's essay "Theoretische Entwürfe über Autorität und Familie" (Theoretical sketches on authority and the family). In so doing, Kracauer brought together in harmony a group of authors who had argued precisely on the significance and shape to be given precisely to such a social psychology as linked the thought of Marx and Freud.[6]

It bears remembering that Fromm's study, *Escape from Freedom*, had just appeared in English in 1941 and was thus more accessible, whereas the volume *Studien zu Autorität und Familie*—edited by Horkheimer with Fromm's assistance and containing the latter's essay—probably exercised a stronger influence on Kracauer's own thought. The volume included a study by Fromm conducted at the Frankfurt Institute of Social Research from 1929 to 1930 which was not to be discovered and reprinted until many years later, namely "Arbeiter und Angestellte am Vorabend des Dritten Reiches" (Wage-earners and salaried staff on the eve of the Third Reich).[7] Fromm had worked the material up into a rough English-language version, which Wolfgang Bonss reedited in 1980 and brought out with a critical commentary.

Kracauer commenced his phenomenological studies on the "white-collar workers" in precisely the same year in which Fromm and his colleagues at the Frankfurt Institute of Social Research conducted theirs. The goal of the latter, or so Fromm wrote in 1937, was: "to collect data on opinions, ways of life and attitudes among workers and white-collar workers. We wanted to gain an impression of what books they read, of how they furnish their apartments and what their favorite theater plays and films were. We were interested in what and in whom they believed, what they had to say on topics such as women at work, bringing children up, and rationalization in the workplace and how they regarded their colleagues and superiors."[8]

This information from 1937 would seem to be of relevance given that Fromm, like Kracauer, addressed the question why the Nazis came to power despite the fact that in elections and mass demonstrations prior to 1933 it was the left-wing parties that had taken center stage. Fromm came to the conclusion that political opinions were fluid among a large section of the electorate and followers of political parties; in other words, the electorate only identified closely with particular political agendas or notions of democracy in specific regards, whereas other aspects of their views were open to seizure by the Nazis. A KPD voter prior to 1933 might have gone along with anticapitalist rhetoric, but owing to his personal view of life might react with rejection and fear to calls for emancipation and freedom. In other words, his anticapitalist sentiment might be satisfied by the National *Socialists* and he would be able to slot himself into a disciplinarian, fear-reducing system of order. Such a change, based on personal emotions, formed the main focus of Fromm's study. Some of the points of overlap between Kracauer and Fromm are interesting because a large section of Kracauer's study is devoted to precisely this fluid, fractured type—a character whom Kracauer convincingly shows to exist in the scenarios portrayed in film during the Weimar Republic.

At this juncture, we must protect Kracauer against the frequently voiced criticism that he was deterministic, jumping from the psychological dispositions of individuals by mysterious leaps and bounds to some collective character he then considered the decisive motor of history. First, we should not construe the Freudian-Marxian social psychology of the 1920s and 1930s as having been deterministic. At most, we could portray the paradigm developed there and exhibited by all such thinkers (irrespective of the school of thinking to which they belonged) in the following manner. Modern societies can only function because they have transformed original rule by force into self-subservience on the part of their members. This self-subjugation extends into the members' very subjectivity and consequently requires the latters' emotional agreement. Precisely the element of freedom in modern societies thus presumes control in a double sense. In the *Dialectic of Enlightenment*, the emphasis is on an ostensibly ineluctable antagonism of natural instinct and an instrumental-rational imperative for self-preservation. In the writings of later champions of a psychology of the Ego (and Fromm was to become one of them), the main claim is that the process of civilization by

79

means of rationalization helped Ego development—i.e., subjectivity is regarded as an historico-cultural entity. These two views were to fuel the debate specifically where, in addition, the theory suggested that the aesthetic dwelled in an autonomous sphere. At least in theoretical terms, in his study Kracauer views films primarily not as aesthetic material, but as cultural symbols in which the subjective characters that are developed function as markers for the collective identity. We would therefore not do Kracauer an injustice if we define his approach in line with a social psychology with roots in a cultural anthropology. It may be fashionable to object that such methods as are derived from sociological views are a priori simplifying—but such objections can hardly be taken seriously. At best, such a method could be examined to test for internal flaws in its construction with regard to the categories developed and its empirical reach.

Philosophically speaking, objections can be raised at the level of the underlying concept of "mentality," according to which all of a person's actions have a mental basis in perception, sensation, and emotions. The latter are therefore considered not only the "other," obverse side of rationality but also a constitutive part of thought. Anyone who accepts this theory will construe the links between psychology and sociology as going beyond the one being merely an addition to the other, even if to the exclusion of other disciplines. Instead, mentality is construed as a bundle of mental dispositions rooted in the thought, feeling, and wishes of a person. Indeed, such a theory would perhaps fit better in Kracauer's attempt to justify his approach than it does in classical social psychology, which has to achieve a qualitative jump from individual to collective subject. For Kracauer does not analyze individuals or collective subjects, but artifacts he understands as symbols that convey dispositions.

He defends himself against the objection that the concept of mentality forms the basis for an ahistorical national character when he says: "Scientific convention has it that in the chain of motivations national characteristics are effects rather than causes—effects of natural surroundings, historic experiences, economic and social conditions. . . . Effects may at any time turn into spontaneous causes. Notwithstanding their derivative character, psychological tendencies often assume independent life, and, instead of automatically changing with ever-changing circumstances, become themselves essential springs of historical evolution."[9]

However, in the theoretical introduction in which he presents his concept of psychological history, we encounter formulations that not only suggest Kracauer takes deterministic shortcuts but provide evidence for this. On occasion, he even contradicts himself. What at one point is a dynamic "ability" dependent on various factors he elsewhere considers a necessary "imperative." What I find more interesting than this would be an interpretation that takes Kracauer's own strong arguments seriously instead of focusing merely on his weaknesses, and I shall therefore address his strengths.

Films, he writes, are "visible hieroglyphs" of the "unseen dynamics of human relations."[10] Precisely because films are manifest in a specific way in images over and above the stories they narrate, they "are more or less characteristic of the inner life of the nation from which the films emerge."[11]

Kracauer argues on two levels when finding justifications for the special status of film as an epistemic screen onto which national introspection is projected. On the one hand, he refers to the collective production process involved in the making of films and which causes individual dispositions to blend to form a joint disposition. On the other, he resorts to a hypothesis from film theory that later permeated his *Theory of Film*.

All possible phenomena of everyday life and the different segments of culture contain information on the mentality that "extend more or less below the dimension of consciousness. . . . But the medium of the screen exceeds these sources in inclusiveness."[12] How should we understand this notion of film's "inclusiveness"? Kracauer refers in this context to an essay by Erwin Panofsky, which he, however, quotes together with items that are part of the general repertoire of film theory: "In a movie theater. . . . the spectator has a fixed seat, but only physically. . . . Aesthetically, he is in permanent motion, as his eye identifies itself with the lens of the camera which permanently shifts in distance and direction. And the space presented to the spectator is as movable as the spectator is himself. Not only do solid bodies move in space, but space itself moves, changing, turning, dissolving and recrystallizing."[13]

81

By virtue of this spatial mobility, films already include "casual configurations of human bodies and inanimate objects, and an endless succession of unobtrusive phenomena," irrespective of whether they are fictional or documentary. It is this "imperceptible surface data" that first makes films "clues" to "hidden mental processes."[14] Fully in keeping with Béla Balázs' early film theory of the "visible man" and Benjamin's hypothesis on the "visual unconscious" only visible to the camera, Kracauer understands the aesthetic theory of film to be "inclusive"—and this also means in the sense that film disclosed the world. For the visible world manifests itself in the "surface data." In this context, Kracauer talks of films reflecting the world. Some have taken this to mean that Kracauer had a simplistic Marxist base/superstructure scheme in mind. This hardly seems plausible given that Kracauer endeavors to tackle an epistemological problem when he assumes that films do not reflect the social world in the form in which it has become second nature, but instead present the physical world in its facticity, that is, in the manner in which it occurs in objects. This idea, and it forms the basis of his *Theory of Film*, refers in other words to those visible phenomena film uses as legible hieroglyphs. In particular, the dynamics of human relationships first come into view in spontaneous expression and to this extent, film exhibits a profound psychological density.

There is a second important side to the film theory, given its direct reference to a media-specific theory of identification; Kracauer does not go into this any further at this juncture, even though it also has a bearing on social psychology. For it is precisely the viewer's invariable identification with the perspective of the camera that makes film so permeable for collective processes. If one takes these two sides to the argument, then we can focus more closely on the issue that Kracauer raised in terms of social psychology: namely whether there are specific social mentalities over and above any assumption of some macro-subject whose voice is the collective.

Kracauer subdivides the empirical material, i.e., the overall body of films, into four historical sections, which he classifies in historiographical terms: the "Archaic Period" (1895–1918); the "Postwar Period" (1918–24); the "Stabilized Period" (1924–29); the "Pre-Hitler Period" (1930–33). These four periods are in turn subdivided into sections numbered 1 through 21, each of which has a title describing one specific motif. These subsections analyze groups of films in part by analyses of exemplary individual cases and in part with respect to an overall genre. It is in these subsections that Kracauer develops the main hypotheses of his book—rather than in the sequencing of the four generalizing and chronologically defined main chapters.

The "Archaic Period" is characterized by a plurality in international film based on a division of tasks in line with the different needs of the cinema-going public. The lack of comedy in Germany, say, is offset by the French and U.S. slapsticks who internalize notions of equality down to the very details of their body language. They are the Calamity Janes who come lucky; contingency and coincidence, which, after all, do not have anything to do with origins or salary levels, are at hand to help. Such an ironic attitude to life is not one of the Germans' talents, who "tended to discredit the notion of luck in favor of that of fate."[15] The decisive hypothesis is then presented as the "foreboding" under which Kracauer subsumes four films: *Der Student von Prag* (The student of Prague) (1913), *Der Golem* (The Golem) (1915), *Homunculus* (1916), and *Der Andere* (The other) (1913). He sees the four as examples for the inner propensity among members of the German middle classes to have a split consciousness. He holds that this is reflected in their preference for purely imaginary topics in which the creation of an artificial human or the assumption of *another* role allows us to see the lack of stability in their own social and psychological identity. What they experience with the threat to their own identity by some mirror images detached from them—by artificial doppelgänger or split-off sections of their own Egos—is a traumatized interior that completely detracts from the material conditions under which it arose. Kracauer regards this split of inner from outer worlds in the pathological imagination as the foreboding of those manic political solutions that were later to seize hold of the masses.

The "Postwar Period" begins with the "shock of freedom," which for a short time unleashes fantasies, only for these to be dashed with the failure of the 1918 revolution and then banished to the realm of the imaginary. The preference for the historical and the exotic thus coincides with the "foreboding" of an imagination split off from political action. The analysis thus suggests that the "foreboding" leads to the blossoming of Expressionist film, which Kracauer then proceeds to investigate with the example of Robert Wiene's *Das Cabinet des Dr. Caligari* (Cabinet of Dr. Caligari).

Kracauer summarizes some of the pronounced motifs and tendencies in the film at the beginning of his chapter devoted to "Destiny" as follows: "In its attempt to reconsider the foundations of the self, German imagination did not confine itself to elaborating upon tyranny, but also inquired into what might happen if tyranny were rejected as a pattern of life. There seemed a sole alternative: for the world to turn into a chaos with all passions and instincts breaking loose. . . . In this plight contemporaneous imagination resorted to the ancient concept of Fate. . . . As an outcome of superior necessity doom at least had grandeur."[16]

Kracauer goes on to trace and uncover this denouement by means of the drama of tragic destiny presented in some Fritz Lang films. Precisely because the latter was an exceptional director, he was exceptionally able to orchestrate those emotions the medium so masterfully "included." The analysis Kracauer gives of the Lang films shows how Kracauer operates with a latent concept of ideology that goes against the grain of any normative concept of aesthetics. The comfortable equation of the beautiful with the true and the good as espoused by idealistic aesthetics is not something for Kracauer. Instead, he considers it incontrovertibly scandalous that Lang succeeded in making aesthetically superior films even though they were full of dubious ideological premises. The boundaries of aesthetic playfulness—where the substance of reality is "sublated"—become osmotically permeable the moment the imaginary becomes a target of politics. Kracauer does not give a normative answer to the trenchant question as to the political and moral implications of the aesthetic. Indeed, this has continued to be a key question down to the present day. Instead, he opts for a descriptive answer referring to the specific historical form of the inextricability, as in this analysis of a motif in Lang's film *Der müde Tod* (Destiny): "It is as if the visuals were calculated to impress the adamant, awe-inspiring nature of Fate upon the mind. Besides hiding the sky, the huge wall Death has erected runs parallel with the screen, so that no vanishing lines allow an estimate of the wall's extent. When the girl is standing before it, the contrast between its immensity and her tiny figure symbolizes Fate as inaccessible to human entreaties. This inaccessibility is also denoted by the innumerable steps the girl ascends to meet Death."[17]

The chapters "Mute Chaos" and "From Rebellion to Submission" further unravel this sociopsychological motif of a rebellion that was brought up short and which after a brief phase of fearful chaos submitted to an authoritarian leader figure. Examples of this include the films on Frederick the Great, who was indeed to become the historical projection screen for the Nazi film.

Phenomenologically speaking, the "Stabilizing Period" is characterized by general "paralysis," by "frozen ground," and the "decline" that set in once a whole series of filmmakers left for the United States. The three groups of films all participate, if in different ways, in the paralysis that resulted from the fact that democratization only took place on the surface after the failure of the revolution and was hardly internalized by large sections of the population. Stereotype comedies and dramas were the order of the day.

By far the most interesting is the third group, which took the stage as "new realism" and which includes "montage" as well as films that were part of New Objectivity and presented a cross-section of reality. Kracauer distinguishes in this context between two currents in New Objectivity, "a romanticizing right wing and a left wing 'bearing a socialist flavor'."[18] The former is based on a one-sided faith in technology tied to technical-economic progress—without simultaneous social progress. Kracauer construes this group to include G. W. Pabst's psychoanalytical film *Geheimnisse einer Seele* (Secrets of a soul), which he regards as an example of how a commercial, psychologistic approach infatuated with the technical opportunities the medium offered overcomes the fraught emotional processes by purely technical means, rather than, as it claims, analyzing them. The opposite trend asserted itself in a few cases, and the 1928 elections in Germany with their massive victories by the left-wing parties seemed to herald a change. However, Kracauer argues, this failed to break through the general paralysis and was to form only a "brief reveille." By contrast, the program of stabilization ushered in by functionalist modernization and simultaneous political stagnation soon established itself.

The "Pre-Hitler Period" was initiated by two external factors: the Great Depression of 1929, with its well-known consequences, and the introduction of the talking movie. The latter led initially to an over-determination of the image by the soundtrack and then to a constriction of the "inclusiveness" that Kracauer had believed provided the basis for his analysis of a mentality in the first place. The prevalent trend was to produce optimistic comedies with musical soundtracks that once and for all carried the spectators off into a fairy-tale world, which they praised as being every-day. Here we find the precursors and heroes of the trends in the Nazi entertainment film industry: "Each Albers film filled the houses in proletarian quarters as well as on Kurfürstendamm. This human dynamo with the heart of gold embodied on the screen what everyone wished to be in life."[19]

However, in the "Pre-Hitler Period," trends in German film polarized into two main groupings that were not particularly structured in terms of ambivalence. In the study, Kracauer again turns to Fritz Lang films, above all *M—eine Stadt sucht einen Mörder* (M—Murderer among Us). The first trend is, he suggests, borne out by people with the "tumbler attitude" of Biberkopf in Piel Jutzi's film of Alfred Döblin's *Berlin Alexanderplatz* and Leontine Sagan's *Mädchen in Uniform*. In the latter film, light is shed on the authoritarian structures of life in a boarding school from the vantage point of the love between a teacher and her girl pupil. The film rightly later became an absolute cult film in lesbian cinema. In contrast to this trend of soft-spoken films that foregrounded the subjectivity of people, the "national epic" endeavored to present domineering individuals on screen as early leader figures—Luis Trenker was one of the most popular actors in such roles. The production of so-called Prussian films in which the battles and martial heroes of Prussian history were presented as the allegories and forerunners of the Nazis rocketed: "It all was as it had been on the screen. The dark premonitions of a final doom were also fulfilled."[20]

This rough outline of the way Kracauer groups his empirical material on film history probably shows where those pivotal points are that then sparked the controversy surrounding the book. Above all, there are great differences in how we should regard the book's rating of films. Even if the reader is prepared to analyze the methodological approach and the rough trends given in it, it is hard to follow all of Kracauer's aesthetic and political judgments. (I do not wish to go into the individual differences and the debate on Kracauer's assessments of films, such as those of Pabst, at this point.)

Moreover, it bears considering that these sections not only investigate German film but cinema as a whole. In the process, analyses of spectator behavior are just as important as are the background to specific film productions. Even if some of the examples Kracauer provides are outdated in view of later research into film history, the "physiognomic" traits of the epoch Kracauer studied by means of these films are still readily discernible.

What is new about Kracauer's study is not that he accords the films normative or social contents but that he derives specific formal patterns from them which he sees as cultural symbols in the sense of undoubted and firmly rooted interpretative and behavioral patterns. He "sees" these symbols quite literally, for, on the one hand, he considers filmic hieroglyphs to be the visible names of things and constellations of events and therefore "sees" films *as* hieroglyphs. On the other, *in* these films he "sees" those concrete patterns he then deciphers *as* hieroglyphs. In order to describe Kracauer's method of analyzing film we need to presume that it is based on these two different figures of a form of visual cognition.

What Kracauer does, and this has annoyed many a commentator since, is to construct an exceptionally strong theory of the meaning of film. Thus, methodological objections to Kracauer's *Caligari* have been formulated not only in terms of a critique of social psychology but also as a critique of the implicit theory of filmic signification on which it is based. It is fair to say that the best sections of *Caligari* are—and this runs counter to the traditional, untenable view of it—an attempt (1) to derive from the formal properties of films (2) mental patterns, which are then (3) subjected to a sociopsychological interpretation. It precisely does not constitute an attempt to grasp contents as significant narratives. Kracauer takes the circular aperture to be a mental symbol of chaos—and only then does he go on to glean from this evident preference for chaos a sociopsychological interpretation which states that there we find a regressive flight from freedom into an anarchistic chaos, rendering action impossible. The mental structure of the circle—which proves in the case of the circular aperture to be a vortex and chaos—alludes to the motif of the organ-grinder at fairgrounds, and, for Kracauer, it is an element of regression in a literary notion of freedom that goes against the grain of its political dimension of free action.

Needless to say, such a form of methodological attribution of signification and its subsequent analysis can be attacked from the widest variety of positions in film theory and theories of signification. However, the entire complex cannot be simply regarded as naïveté on Kracauer's part, for his examples are simply far too detailed. And even if there are repeated inaccuracies on his part, *Caligari* nevertheless set certain standards and can still be accepted as such.

The interweaving of contents, techniques, and form to make up one motif overlaps in fact with another methodological and theoretical approach to analyzing images with which Kracauer was familiar. Indeed, what I have in mind is not even the quotation from the writings of the esteemed art historian Erwin Panofsky, which Kracauer places prominently in his introduction. Rather, there are methodological parallels worthy of investigation. Volker Breidecker has outlined the contact between Panofsky and Kracauer—it developed, while Kracauer was in exile in the United States, into a vigorous and intensive exchange of views—specifically with regard to this strange interweaving of form and content. Kracauer's methodological contribution to empirical sociology consists of the qualitative radical twist he gives to content analysis. After all, he goes so far as to treat negative findings as valid units of analysis and proceeds to infer statements from these units—in other words, to his mind what is *not* said is as important as what *is* said. This procedure seems plausible and hardly surprising if seen against the backdrop of experience of everyday communication. However, in the framework of the decidedly positivistic and quantifying methodology of the day it was quite pioneering. Moreover, Panofsky's iconology was also not far removed from Kracauer's preference for visual motifs—we could term them standing images the way sociologists speak of "standing motifs." In other words, they are motifs that persist, frequently recur, and seem to be so obdurate as to confound the opinion that meaning is merely contingent. And for Kracauer those concealed motifs are historically significant, just as for

Panofsky such motifs would be culturally significant. What I have in mind here are those motifs which, having been detached from their origins, are to be encountered on the surface of things and phenomena. Accordingly, Kracauer commented in a letter to Panovsky on the latter's study of Dürer with words that would have perfectly fitted his own oeuvre:

> That is how you compose your interpretation of "Melancholy." . . . It is as if the engraving was an almost insurmountable fortress which you surround from all sides and then ardently besiege, until the fortress no longer endures the repeated waves of interpretative motifs and runs up the white flag. . . . Only such a siege will get to the inner world of the picture: only once it has taken place, can your final comment that melancholy is "a spiritual self-portrait of Dürer" shine forth in all its luminosity. It is as if we were looking through a miniature hole in the wall at an immeasurably large landscape.[21]

Latent in this entire passage is a sort of self-recognition, only manifest clearly in the spiraling mention of the "spiritual self-portrait"—something the interpreter has just as much a part of as does the artist who presents himself and is thus interpreted. In the thought of both Panofsky and Kracauer, we constantly encounter an awareness of the problem of historical density (or distance) to a historical object and how to interpret the present—a subject to which the two men frequently returned in their correspondence on *Caligari*.[22] We should not underestimate the role of biography and autobiography in Kracauer's work, over and above the bourgeois mode of biography he once so sharply criticized. This may also be connected with the fact that experiences in one's own biography may be inscribed in memory as "documents" of major historical events. Beyond all polemics of the stylized biographies of "great men" such as those written by Emil Ludwig, the concept of experience plays a key role here, a concept otherwise encountered primarily in the writings of Adorno. Debates in recent years have focused on whether, now that we have bid farewell to auteur theory and the history of philosophy, such undertakings even tackle meaningful questions. This shall remain a moot point here. Suffice it to say that Kracauer himself reflected on many aspects of the issue in his book on history, first published posthumously.

As is the case when addressing many texts that structurally are based on the understanding of signification afforded by psychoanalysis, it is easy when focusing on *Caligari* to treat individual interpretations skeptically. They all depend on an immense degree of assumed coherence—with regard to not only the collective on which they rest, and historicity, but also the textual construction, i.e., that which is respectively interpreted as a coherent text. The objection that despite Kracauer's conscious rejection of teleological views of history, the book suffers from a structure based far too strongly on knowledge acquired after the event and thus construes all German history as the precursor of the Third Reich, is only partially true. Kracauer knows all too well that there are no "laws" of history from which we can deduce causal inevitabilities, that other narrative contexts are imaginable from which we could deduce other links. However, the vanishing point of his study is the Nazi present and not the many possible other histories or courses history could have taken.

Kracauer's literary talents emerge in the polemical tone found in many passages in his *Caligari*. He pours scorn, for example, on those of the Germans' preferences he adumbrates. The vivid picture he paints in such animated descriptions of fictitious persons and scenarios has as its sounding board the hypothesis that art and life blend unfavorably in the Nazi aestheticization of politics. At an early date, he detects the pathological and manic traits of this combination in the films' broken figures. Taking the example of Fritz Lang's films, Kracauer underlines the ambivalences in which even those who did not concur with the Nazis' nomenclature seem to have become embroiled. Thus, he reads the second Mabuse film as an interesting interim piece, an example of that interrupted rebellion which eventually bends down to the Fuehrer. Kracauer writes:

> Dr. Goebbels undoubtedly knew why he banned the film. However, it is hard to believe that the average German audiences would have grasped the analogy between the gang of screen criminals and the Hitler gang. And had they even been aware of it, they would not have felt particularly encouraged to stand up against the Nazis, for Lang is so exclusively concerned with highlighting the magic spell of Mabuse and Baum that his film mirrors their demoniac irresistibility rather than the inner supe-

riority of their opponents. . . . This anti-Nazi film betrays the power of Nazi spirit over minds insufficiently equipped to counter its peculiar fascination.[23]

Perhaps we should add that Lang himself wished his film to be understood as an allegory on the Nazis and that Kracauer's proposal that there was a secret coherence at work in it was not exactly commonplace at the time. This gives us more of a sense of how radical his position was. However, this radical thrust earned him all the worse a reputation for having lit the fire of the world spirit in keeping with Hegel's philosophy of history.

Even the critical reviews on the occasion of the publication of the book in the United States emphasize that perhaps the methodological questions the book implicitly raises and tackles are more interesting than the sociopsychological and contemporaneous diagnoses it provides by way of empirical results. These are probably too close to debates of the day on the "special path" Germany had taken with regard to the German "subject" and history to be surprising—and they adhere too closely to the stereotypes that were found in the films. Thus, the reviewers often express disappointment at not having learned anything essentially new other, perhaps, than the fact that precisely a new method was offered on how to read films as sociopsychological hieroglyphs. The retrospective diagnosis on the Hitler period will always be slightly disappointing, as it moves, after all, in terrain in which everyone had made their own experiences. It is nevertheless interesting that some of the reviewers rightly point out that the diagnostic audacity of the procedure should be assessed less with regard to *Caligari* and more to the study *Propaganda and the Nazi War Film* written in 1942 and published with it. One commentator wrote at the time:

> What makes Kracauer's book so important is that it sets a new pattern for analysing films, wherein the analyser approaches the film as a physician approaches a patient . . . Kracauer's analysis of German propaganda films . . . originally issued in 1942 to serve the purposes of psychological warfare, presents for the first time a scientific method for determining the propaganda as factor in films. . . . He has accomplished here a kind of film

91

atom-smashing and in this instance the cunningly concealed lies and distortions of Nazi film makers have dissolved in the "acid" Kracauer has prepared for them so that they are revealed for the lies and distortions that they are.[24]

The study of war propaganda is one of the fields in empirical and political sociology in the United States in which emigrants were employed thanks to their superior knowledge of the subject matter and empathy with regard to cultural specifics and languages. Alongside Kracauer, Marcuse, Lowenthal, Lazarsfeld, and many other of his friends worked on projects devoted to defending against propaganda. Quite apart from the political import of Kracauer's work at the time— it was written in the framework of "psychological warfare"—he continued to try and devise a method for analyzing positive and negative forms of influence after 1945, when anti-Semitism among the homecoming GIs seemed to pose a problem. Kracauer took part in the large-scale anti-Semitism project run by Max Horkheimer on behalf of the American Jewish Committee. He was not only present at countless discussions but also participated actively in preparing the so-called test film that was to be screened at group discussions in order to stimulate debate. This unique project prompted a lively ongoing exchange of views up until Kracauer's late seventies on how stereotypes and prejudices function prior to, in, and through mass cultural media and specifically in film.

The test film was never shot, but numerous scripts were written, partly with Kracauer's involvement. Moreover, the entire debate on filmic representation of Jews and anti-Semites in film was taken a step further in the discussion on Edward Dmytryk's film *Crossfire*, which was deliberately planned by the studio in question as a political counter-toxin to the prevalent anti-Semitism. It came out in 1947—at the same time as Kracauer's book, attesting to the continuity of the problems it addressed in Kracauer's thought.[25]

It is interesting to note the criticisms voiced by Martha Wolfenstein and Nathan Leites in this context; both were leading mass communications researchers and had brought out an investigation of film with a psychoanalytic thrust in 1950 titled *Movies: A Psychological Study*. The short review of Kracauer they published in *Psychoanalyti-*

cal Quarterly pointed out that Kracauer failed to provide a comparative study in which the empirical claims on specific national characteristics were relativized or at least presented in a more differentiated fashion against a comparative background. They therefore asked what the "national" differences were in view of the fact that in U.S. horror films mad citizens seized power. Nevertheless, they did not contest that it might be the nuances that revealed the differences concerned and stated that Kracauer had made "the first large-scale attempt to describe and interpret films as cultural data."[26] Had they followed Kracauer's overall work more carefully, they would have come across an article on the problem published in 1946 in *Commentary* titled "Hollywood's Terror Films: Do They Reflect an American State of Mind?"[27]

The answer Kracauer gave was intended to provide a diagnosis of his epoch and regards such films as we would probably tend to call film noir today as ambiguous reflections of moral and cruel condemnations of history in Europe and of their U.S. counterparts. Kracauer writes: "That panic which in the anti-Nazi films was characterized as peculiar to the atmosphere of life under Hitler now saturates the whole world."[28] The fear and terrorized horror that had become a symbol of Modernity in Kafka's novels is wedded in Kracauer's mind with the experience of mass destruction in Europe.[29] Kracauer focused on this sociopsychological dual function of playful sublation of violence and of rendering it a behavioral routine in a small piece titled "The execution of *Mary Queen of Scots*," a film produced in 1895, where he elucidates the affinity of cinema to horror.[30]

Wolfenstein and Leites fail to even remotely discuss the dilemmas perhaps shared by applied psychoanalysis, film theory, and social psychology, and their criticism of Kracauer's unjustified conclusions in which "inanimate objects stand for 'mute instincts'"[31] remains unsubstantiated—the main objection they raise to the book they are reviewing.[32] The general problems of psychoanalytical interpretations can by no means give leverage on applied psychoanalysis but have meanwhile been seen to relate also to a wide spectrum, including the very core of the psychoanalytical paradigm. To this extent, much in Kracauer's book now seems outdated, even though it was quite pioneering at the time. For all the criticism of psychoanalysis, we should not forget that it is precisely the psychoanalytical method of interpretation which for the first time calls for that "inclusiveness" Kracauer accords film. In the form of the free-floating attention the analyst pays to coincidental remarks, the method is deployed in order to illuminate the "dynamics of human relations" for a few seconds in a film.

One of the few historians who takes film seriously as a bearer of signification is Marc Ferro, a member of the French Annales school. In his brief but important statement, he takes up Kracauer's work, even if he does not quote from it:

> We have already seen that a film on the present age can be a work on history, or, to be more precise, on counter-history, as the contents always exceed the image, be it fiction or not. . . . This counter-analysis can take place at various levels: initially in the form of a museum of gestures, of objects and of forms of social behavior; then as a counter-analysis of social structures and forms of organization—above all in non-documentary films that are not intended to provide information. And, finally, there are films in which the explicit will to reveal the secret functional mechanisms of society . . . leads to the creation of a work of counter-history which attracts the criticism of all institutional systems.[33]

Like Kracauer, Ferro deploys a notion of a museum of gestures beneath the surface—for Kracauer, this was the product of film's "inclusiveness." The normatively defined conception of counter-history as a critical interpretation of the question of domination is something Kracauer would not so easily subscribe to. He remains an advocate of Critical Theory in construing counter-history not just as mere opposition to the dominant system but also, on the one hand, as an epistemic feature of the medium and, on the other, as resembling all other cultural artifacts in that it is forever on the verge of becoming affirmative. However, as an expressive medium such counter-history should be approached, he suggests, primarily not with a view to normative aspects. In this regard, historians of the cinema still have much to learn from Kracauer.

Space, Time, and Apparatus:
The Optical Medium "Theory of Film"

WE HAVE SEEN that *From Caligari to Hitler* is not just a book that refers to the history of film. It is likewise the outline of an implicit history of the decline of the individual (on which the new masses are based) and the subject's regression into subordination. This development, Kracauer believes, causes Modernity to break off, having only half fulfilled its potential. It therefore comes as no surprise that *Theory of Film* is equally not just what its title suggests, but also an irritating statement on the visibility of the world as well as the resulting cognitive and moral opportunities and obligations. *Theory of Film* stands out for the numerous different tasks its author expects one single medium to square up to. Indeed, it is no coincidence that he took up some of the ideas adumbrated there in his later book on a theory of history.

Kracauer was planning a material aesthetics and a theory of film well before the publication of *Theory of Film*. He wrote to Adorno in February 1949: "In this book, again, film will only be an excuse. I wish to show what aesthetic laws and *affinities* to certain themes are developed by a medium which is fully the product of an age in which scientific interest in the links between the smallest elements is increasingly surpassing the dynamism of major ideas that embrace the whole human being, and 'transcending' our sensitivity to such ideas."[1]

In these remarks, Kracauer describes film as a type of "force demoliteur" that rejects the totalizing attempt of systematic and speculative thought in the tradition of the Enlightenment. Indeed, we can sense here not only his old preference for the micrological (a love shared by Adorno), but also an interest in innovative philosophical positions from which a new underpinning for materialism could be created.

95

In the above-quoted letter, Kracauer continued: "Or, to couch it in the language of film: the aesthetics of film can be assigned to an epoch in which the old 'long-shot' perspective, which believed that it in some way focused on the absolute, is replaced by a 'close-up' perspective, which instead sheds light on the meaning of individuated things, of the fragment."[2]

In other words, Kracauer is again concerned to grasp an entire "epoch" by means of one of its surface-level expressions. However, the epoch in question is something that can no longer be recorded by means of a totalizing panoramic perspective; instead, he suggests, only by means of individual close-ups will it be possible to illuminate something, just as spotlights "shed light" on something and therefore set it off against a dark background or render visible something we have overlooked. This idea of rendering things visible—and it runs like a red thread through Kracauer's thought at the time—contains the philosophical concept behind the entire book. For Kracauer repeatedly asserts that film, thanks to its photographic properties, has a specific ability that distinguishes it from other aesthetic media. "Photographic properties" are understood here as the ability to render physical reality visible. This ability is a substantive quality of film and results from its specific filmic characteristics. However, Kracauer continues, the ability must first be enacted. Put differently, the ability to render things visible should by no means be understood to automatically occur in all films in the sense of some technical given. Rather, things are rendered visible if the requisite perceptual capacity exists.

Kracauer defines photographic and filmic images (I shall return to the difference below) by means of a tripartite semiotic figure: it is the infinite variety of the physical, material world that forms the reservoir of referential objects to which our perception then relates. Here, Kracauer brings two different operations into play: one is technical, stemming from the fundamentals of the camera (lens, film, light sensitivity), the other personal, resulting from the sensory, cultural, and psychological disposition of the perceptual apparatus. These two modes can, in turn, be subdivided into two trends: one appropriates reality, the other gives it a form. Kracauer is sure that objections will be raised against the substantialist notion inherent in these justifications and as a consequence always constrains them somewhat. But we should not let this deceive us, for he repeatedly comes back to the properties of the medium we summarized above. For this reason, he faced the notorious objection that he was not only a "curious" or "abysmally profound realist," but even a "normative realist," who derived aesthetic principles from an ontology of the photographic medium, i.e., from its materialized properties. Yet how does Kracauer justify this philosophical realism? The strong claims it puts forward as regards the reference of film to reality and on the truth of the subsequent filmic image have, after all, been the subject of much discussion over the last fifty years. And how can Kracauer reconcile his skepticism toward totalizing perspectives with this strong claim? Moreover, the question arises, as to how far Kracauer left the conceptual frames of the prewar period behind him in *Theory of Film*, replacing it with a new philosophical option. The debate on how to appraise his work—and it is one that has been fought quite fiercely in recent literature on Kracauer—hinges not least on these questions.[3]

Here, at the latest, it becomes necessary to glance back if we are to obtain a position from which we can move forward. We need to resort to Kracauer's early essay on photography, which not only preempts some of the motifs of *Theory of Film*, but also addresses questions that then take center stage in *History: The Last Things before the Last*. In the essay, published in 1927, Kracauer presented paradoxes of photography that still have to be tackled by any attempt in theoretical reflection on photography today.

THE PARADOX OF TIME AND SPACE IN THE PHOTOGRAPHIC IMAGE

We can briefly summarize this paradox as follows: it is the paradox between the spatialized presence of the object in the photograph and its rigid link to the time the photograph is taken. Adorno once referred, in a letter to Walter Benjamin, to this obverse side to the prohibition on producing graven images as the point where reification

97

switches over into forgetting: "For all reification is forgetting: objects become like things the moment they are fixed in time without actually being present in all their parts: where some part of them is forgotten."[4]

Taking the dialectic of remembrance and forgetting as the pivot of how we are aware of history in memory, Kracauer elaborates on the points of reference between the moment in which the photograph is taken and that in which we look at it. In his essay on photography he therefore brought together two photos, one of the "film diva," the other of a "grandmother." He wrote:

> This is what the *film diva* looks like. She is twenty-four years old, featured on the cover of an illustrated magazine, standing in front of the Hotel Excelsior on the Lido. The date is September. If one were to look through a magnifying glass one could make out the grain, the millions of little dots that constitute the diva, the waves, and the hotel. The picture, however, refers not to the dot matrix but to the living diva on the Lido. Time: the present. The caption calls her demonic: our demonic diva. . . . Everyone recognizes her with delight, since everyone has already seen the original on the screen. It is such a good likeness that she cannot be confused with anyone else.[5]

With regard to the photograph of grandmother, the question arises as to the perspective from which the viewer perceives it. The viewer assumed by Kracauer knows the "object" photographed not from memories of other reproductions, and not from his own imagination, but nevertheless wishes to create a historical continuum, with the grandmother at one end and the photograph of her as a young girl at the other. Kracauer therefore continues: "This is what grandmother looked like? The photograph, more than sixty years old and already a photograph in the modern sense, depicts her as a young girl of twenty-four. Since photographs are likenesses, this one must have been a likeness as well. It was carefully produced in the studio of a court photographer. But were it not for the oral tradition, the image alone would not have sufficed to reconstruct the grandmother."[6]

In the course of time, the legibility of the photograph, the recognition of its likeness, dwindles. When viewing the photography, we therefore discern the passage of unrecoverable time and "shudder." The photograph buries that which it depicts—"covering it with snow," as it were—because as a medium photography cannot present the "history" of the object photographed. Although the photo reproduces "reality," the latter emerges in the photo only as the spatial fixation of a past moment, in other words, as dead matter.

In light of the above, we can pinpoint an ambivalence in photography, namely its inability to convey that "significance" which structures memory—in other words, the historical significance of the mnemonic image that visually makes up the "history" of a person in our memories. Kracauer describes quite vividly this difference between photographic image and mnemonic image:

> *Memory* encompasses neither the entire spatial appearance of something nor its entire temporal course. Compared to photography, memory's records are full of gaps. The fact that the grandmother was at one time involved in a nasty story that is recounted time and again because people really do not like to talk about her—this does not mean much from the photographer's perspective. He knows every little wrinkle on her face and has noted every date. . . . Photography grasps what is given as a spatial (or temporal) continuum; memory images retain what is given only insofar as it has significance.[7]

In this way, Kracauer initially distinguishes strictly between the two phenomena: namely photography, on the one hand, and significance, history, and art on the other. However, he does not stop there. Some of his formulations already indicate that photography is not to be understood as some more straightforward, less conscious technical medium, some naive empiricism, but, instead, that this difference is what enables photography to possess specific abilities. At the end of his essay, Kracauer inverts cultural criticism's contention that photography remains bound to the surface level compared with the signification with which history is construed in a mnemonic image. In the seventh section of the essay he sketches a historical genesis of symbols, borrowed from Bachofen. "'Symbolism,' Bachofen says, 'like language, sat in nature's lap.'"[8] Kracauer continues: "Bachofen means the genesis of all language and images from interchange with material nature. Bachofen introduces symbols as the reference points that are purely physical and material."[9] The products of an originary relationship to nature, starting with the symbol, give rise to a "series of pictorial representations, of which photography is the last historical stage."[10] Kracauer inserts a moment of dialectical change into the framework of this theory of images, in which the image functions as a sort of indicator for the degree to which people depend on or control nature. This dialectical component enables him to describe photography as a sort of substitute location in Modernity for symbols. He writes: "For long stretches of history, imagistic representations have remained symbols. As long as human beings need them, they continue, in practice, to be dependent on natural conditions, a dependence which determines the visible and corporeal expression of consciousness. It is only with the increasing domination of nature that the image loses its symbolic power."[11]

The change in the structure and significance of images occurs with the shift from symbol to allegory, which makes use of the image as a function of thought. With the increasing domination of nature, humans become more conscious of nature without any longer having to rely on nature being seen through the medium of myths and symbols, or images and allegories for that matter. At this point, nature and image again go different ways. Kracauer states: "Since nature changes in exact correspondence with the particular state of consciousness of a period, the foundation of nature devoid of meaning arises with modern photography."[12] Put differently, it is precisely photography, devoid of memory and incapable of cognitively grasping historical significance or the history of persons, that finds itself at the juncture that is a void, at the point where the potential for a complete dialectic changeover exists. Photography occupies this void and thus makes it the point of archival recording and the point where everyone and everything reverts to "the foundation of nature devoid of meaning."

At this stage in the essay, Kracauer comes up with an enigmatic and utopian trope in order to pinpoint the dialectical moment of complete change. He outlines that "the nature that it failed to penetrate would sit down at the very table that consciousness had abandoned. If this society failed to endure, however, then liberated consciousness would be given an incomparable opportunity. Less enmeshed in the natural bonds than ever before, it could prove its power in dealing with them. The turn to photography is the *go-for-broke game* of history."[13]

In other words, Kracauer is suggesting here that history places all its bets on one card, namely photography, because in the latter, the foundation of nature becomes visible, devoid of superimposed meaning. Thus, photography amounts, on the one hand, to a totalizing procedure, for it can be construed as a "general inventory of a nature that cannot be further reduced," a "comprehensive catalogue." On the other, it bursts asunder the false semblance of a purportedly significant history and leads us into an "inert world," a "world of the dead" that exists completely independently of human beings. With regard to this idea of photography enabling us to overcome a reified history, Kracauer then elaborates on the temporal dimension of order. He brings Kafka into the argument and summarizes his conception by covert analogy to a figure in Jewish mysticism, namely the notion that it is therefore "incumbent on consciousness to establish the *provisional status* of all given configurations, and perhaps even to awaken an inkling of the right order of the inventory of nature."[14]

This cold glance at the dead world of things is not instilled with significance simply by having a monogram embroidered onto it, and therefore grants us that freedom such as is rendered possible by new montages of things that are the detritus of history. Consequently, at the end of the essay on photography, Kracauer presents film as the force that can "stir up" playful projected orders: "The disorder of the detritus reflected in photography cannot be elucidated more clearly than through the suspension of every habitual relationship among the elements of nature. The capacity to stir up the elements of nature is one of the possibilities of film."[15]

Following this outline of Kracauer's essay on photography we can now ask whether the hypotheses put forward there were absorbed into his later theory of film or were first fundamentally overhauled. This question could not only be raised with reference to how Kracauer links photography back to the foundations of nature, but also with regard to the role he assigned to moving images in film and the possibilities of montage.

THEORY OF FILM

Kracauer outlines his agenda in the foreword to the book. It is an agenda featuring various assumptions that concur with those in the essay on photography, expanded now to include an aesthetic concept of material.[16] Kracauer provides a theoretical basis for his film theory by assuming "film is essentially an extension of photography and therefore shares with this medium a marked affinity for the visible world around us. Films come into their own when they record and reveal physical reality."[17]

As in the essay on photography, Kracauer goes on to refer to the subjective conditions for perceiving what has been "revealed." He states quite explicitly that the filmic reality is richer than the everyday perception, that film is a medium for locking into the world, and the world of film is "a flow of random events involving both humans and inanimate objects."[18] We could say here that whereas in photography each and every thing is turned into an inanimate object, presenting time in a spatial dimension, in film, thanks to the presence of motion, another dimension is involved—space is rendered dynamic by means of motion, by instilling objects otherwise fixated in immobile form in photography with motion. Thierry de Duve has described this discrepancy of photography as a paradox of the different perceptual modes by referring to the legendary attempt to document by photographic means a horse with all four hoofs in the air: "For Muybridge's snapshots of a galloping horse demonstrated what the animal's movements were, but did not convey the sensation of their motion."[19]

In his foreword, Kracauer refers expressly to the somatic level in the perception of films, the "movement" of which can only be perceived in the first place by a physical reaction (and is often experienced as a bodily sensation). He speaks of how we "assimilate" the "seemingly non-essential" as a possible way to build a bridge between ourselves and the surface level of the world and things. The path leads from the "corporeal," which cinema helps to "move from 'below' to 'above'."[20] Miriam Hansen has elaborated on how Kracauer assumes a somatically mediated position of the individual as spectator, the in-

dividual complete "with skin and hair," in the book and in his preliminary studies.[21]

At this level, Kracauer's theory of film appears far more modern
than the occasionally over-ornate language, the intrinsic contradictions, and the lack of clarity would suggest. The chapter Kracauer
devotes to the "spectator," by contrast, clearly outlines the latter's
position, for he writes: "Let us assume that, unlike other types of
pictures, film images affect primarily the spectator's senses, engaging
him physiologically before he is in a position to respond intellectu-
ally. . . . Movement is the alpha and omega of the medium. Now the
sight of it seems to have a 'resonance effect,' provoking in the spectator such kinesthetic responses as muscular reflexes, motor impulses,
or the like."[22]

The somatic strand in Kracauer's argumentation is far-ranging. Indeed, it rests on an anthropological approach at the center of which
he locates physiological constitution as the core of human nature.
With reference to the revelatory functions of photographic film, he
avers that the unknown shapes address less our power of reasoning
and more our visceral faculties.

The sensualist theory of filmic perception should not deceive us,
however, into overlooking the fact that here Kracauer again introduces something like an ethics of enjoyment. He describes the distracted, semi-lucid state of spectatorship as a form of meditation before (in a manner reminiscent of Heidegger) then proceeding to offer
an instance of that misplaced enthusing, which prompted such sharp
criticism of the book: "Does the spectator ever succeed in exhausting
the objects he contemplates? There is no end to his wanderings.
Sometimes, though, it may seem to him that, after having probed a
thousand possibilities, he is listening, with all his senses strained, to a
confused murmur. Images begin to sound, and the sounds are again
images. When this indeterminate murmur—the murmur of existence—reaches him, he may be nearest to the unattainable goal."[23]
Kracauer's notion of the thing-in-itself evidently hinges on an existentialist ontology, and film is indeed a medium en route to "existence."

Kracauer clearly turns his back on the theory of photography as a
mirror of reality, instead emphasizing the element of constructivity

and arbitrariness in photography, the degree to which it depends on the spectator's position. In doing so, he takes account of the problems of geometrical projections of three-dimensional objects onto a two-dimensional surface that Arnheim had long since elaborated. Nevertheless, under the heading of "Affinities" he then underlines those aspects of photography essentially caused by its closeness to nature in the raw. He enumerates four such typical affinities: the affinity for unstaged reality, the accentuation of the fortuitous, the suggestion of endlessness, and the affinity for the indeterminate.

Kracauer concedes that films, even more so than photographs, are shaped not just by their realistic tendency but also by their formative tendency. However, he claims that the "fundamental aesthetic principle" of film demands that a specific relationship to the physical world be recognized. We could perhaps say that Kracauer grounds his theory of film on a specific theory of the aesthetic that centers precisely not on some hermetically closed artwork but instead on a specific configuration of sensualism as the basis for a material aesthetics. The pivotal reflection on perception links the position of the producer as subject to that of the spectator as subject. Kracauer thus not only puts forward the aforementioned affinities as the foundations for his theory but also addresses the impact of those characteristics with which he endeavors to grasp the medium and distinguish it from others. Unlike traditional art, what is specific about film is that "truly 'cinematic' films . . . incorporate aspects of physical reality with a view to making us experience them."[24]

"However, the supreme virtue of the camera consists precisely in acting the voyeur."[25] The secret voyeur can also enjoy being witness and "neutral observer" of a quasi-scientific experiment. Irrespective of the role Kracauer accords the camera, it always follows the rule of the "fundamental aesthetic principle" of rendering things visible. As a consequence, the camera alights upon all the areas that are "registered" in advance; in the process, some are "revealed" and opened up to human experience in the medium of the photograph thus produced. To this extent, alongside all the phenomena our gaze and that of the camera spontaneously alight on, all those other things too large or too small, too close or too indistinct to be perceived can also be considered filmic phenomena. This also includes things in the world of the past: "In a flash the camera exposes the paraphernalia of our former existence, stripping them of the significance which originally transfigured them so that they changed from things in their own right into invisible conduits. . . . The thrill of these old films is that they bring us face to face with the inchoate, cocoon-like world whence we come—all the objects, or rather sediments of objects, that were our companions in a pupa state."[26]

Invoking "things in their own right" as the fundamental aesthetic principle of "cinematic films" would appear also to involve those problems associated with a philosophical position according to which it is possible to perceive a "thing-in-itself" prior to any semiotic properties it may have. To avoid such an assumption, Kracauer places an interpreter between us and the thing in itself, namely the camera or the film as a medium. Nevertheless, his approach (which was, as we have seen, already present in the essay on photography) would seem to have introduced a theological theme behind the materialist motif of the "natural foundations of mankind." The implications of this methodology perhaps emerge most clearly when Kracauer resorts to moral constructs when addressing the random contingencies of the natural state.

Thus, taking up the thought of another writer, he introduces the concept of "solidarity of the universe." He bases the idea on the assemblage of events we witness in film, for such scattered events can only be brought together simultaneously in film. This talk of the "solidarity of the universe" is, however, only meaningful as a metaphor for creation—the principles underlying it remain concealed from us, but we know that it is more than mere matter. An analogy would be for us to think of the creation of man from a lump of clay as a theory on biological development and not just a religious myth of creation. The matter from which Kracauer draws the parts of his theory is the theological "matter" of creation, where the thing-in-itself appears as that which God has made and its sensory perception a human achievement. In the process, Kracauer continually gives the camera the perspective of a divine eye. For example, when quoting the Italian director Cavalcanti, he says that, for the camera, actors who are dressed up in historical costumes do not count as roles being played but as actors dressed up, for the camera is "literally-minded."[27]

105

Kracauer's theory of film can be subdivided analytically into three components or areas, namely a *sensualist* aesthetics (adumbrated by means of an analytic of the spectator), a philosophy of the real based on an *existential ontology* (whereby existence is taken as the domain of referential objects), and a redemptive figure based on an *aesthetics of reconciliation* (which Kracauer roots in the specifics of film as a medium). All three areas are based on a notion of experience Kracauer fails to think through in a uniform manner.

In the epilogue to his *Theory of Film*, Kracauer repeats these tropes in his theory and embeds them in a diagnosis of his times, locating them in the context of the general collapse of traditional values, relativism, and abstract thought. Here, the way film accesses the physical world, its somatic enracination, and its indeterminacy (which could protect it against any trammeling to an ideology) all appear as a way of conveying a type of experience that is richer and more comprehensive than can be the respective experience of its parts. The somatic foundations shield film against the barrenness of abstraction; the mediate character of images insulates film against the suggestion of directness; the many perspectives provided by operative montage defend film against modern relativism; and concrete experiences with individual things (which are viewed in a meditative way and not only in a manner conveyed through the media in which we see them) prevent film from falling into the void that was the prior location of the religious. Thus, film teaches us to see the world: in the view it gives, we see through the false and superficial sensuousness and conventionality of things and perceive behind them the material being of things, their raw state of creation.

The flow of life, in which things and the dead are swept away, is arrested by film; it is the "redemption of physical reality."[28] To what end does film redeem it? The idea of redemption, already latent in the notion of "solidarity with the universe," is deeply bound up with Benjamin's call for anamnestic solidarity—for dedicated commemoration of the dead, together with whom we wait for the day when the Messiah will come, the day when the dead are done justice. It is doubtless a notion from the Jewish faith that the dead do not leave earth but are linked in a material continuum with the living, whose support they demand. In Kracauer's attempt to create an aesthetics of reconciliation by redeeming the flow of life in filmic motion pictures, this figure of thought is decidedly present, if in covert form. It shatters the false order into which we have arranged things and the latter become accessible for the first time for a new order, the plan for which we do not know. Only by preserving them can we show our commitment to solidarity with the dead things so that, once revealed, they can shine forth in a different, perhaps more favorable light. The crypto-theological core of Kracauer's notion of the "redemption of physical reality" is shaped by a notion of creation. It is a creation *of which* we must make no image, but which we should instead preserve in its material character. Kracauer's concept of a utopia linked back to ontological properties appears to me to point in this direction. And this was probably the basis for the reserve he showed toward Adorno's version of dialectical thought. He was suspicious of any notion of conceptual mediation. In his critique of Adorno's *Negative Dialectics* Kracauer spoke of an

> unfettered dialectic which eliminates ontology altogether. His rejection of any ontological stipulation in favor of an infinite dialectics which penetrates all concrete things and entities seems inseparable from a certain arbitrariness, an absence of content and direction in these series of material evaluations. The concept of Utopia is then necessarily used by him in a purely formal way, as a borderline concept which at the end invariably emerges like a *deus ex machina*. But Utopian thought only makes sense if it assumes the form of a vision or intuition with a definite content of a sort. Therefore the radical immanence of the dialectical process will not do; some ontological fixations are needed to imbue it with significance and direction.[29]

In this context, it is of interest that Kracauer reacted hesitantly to the events Adorno essayed to address in *Negative Dialectics*. Mass-scale annihilation, which informs Adorno's thought on Auschwitz, is quite anathema to Kracauer. Kracauer refers only once to the existence of concentration camps—in a footnote. And the footnote refers to an essay written by the historian Herbert Butterfield in 1931 (that is, prior to mass annihilation in the death camps), titled "Moral Judgments in History": "Butterfield . . . alludes to this possibility when he says that the (technical) historian may assist the cause of morality by describing, in concrete detail and in an objective manner, a wholesale massacre, the consequence of religious persecution, or the goings-on in a concentration camp. For the rest, Butterfield's idea of technical history itself originates in an intricate mixture of theological and scientific notions."[30]

Kracauer himself takes up the theological motif in an oddly ambiguous manner. This does not seem coincidental, reflecting as it does central motifs in his thinking: redemption through reification, vacillation between phenomenological concretism and theology, the confluence of which remains ontologically disguised in *Theory of Film*. In the text mentioned above, Kracauer paradoxically distances himself from the theological in a manner thoroughly typical of him: "So the question as to the meaningfulness of 'technical history' would seem to be unanswerable. There is only one single argument in its support which I believe to be conclusive. It is a theological argument, though. According to it, the 'complete assemblage of the smallest facts' is required for the reason that nothing should go lost. It is as if the fact-oriented accounts breathed pity with the dead. This vindicates the figure of the *collector*."[31]

Kracauer makes use of the figure of redemption through memory—that is to say, anamnestic solidarity with the dead—in a framework in which people and facts have both to an equal extent become things. It appears as though it is only when the world is petrified in images that it can be deciphered and experienced as having a human face. As indicated by the subtitle—which is likewise the heading of the final chapter—*Theory of Film* is based entirely on "The Redemption of Physical Reality." In this last chapter Kracauer also addresses pictures of the death camps. Under the subtitle "The Head of the Medusa," Kracauer begins with the story of the myth "as we learned it in school." He interprets Pallas Athena's advice to Perseus not to look directly at the dreadful head of the Gorgon, but only at its reflection in the polished shield, to mean "that we do not, and cannot, see actual horrors because they paralyze us with blinding fear; and that we shall know what they look like only by watching images of them which reproduce their true appearance."[32]

Cinema thus functions as the mirror for a nature as horrifying as Medusa's head and in which events take place that "would petrify us were we to encounter them in real life. The film screen is Athena's polished shield."[33] However, according to Kracauer the myth does not stop at the cathartic function of "reflection" as the verification of our own perceptions. Athena, whose advice enables Perseus to behead Medusa, used the captured head to scare off her enemies. "Perseus, the image watcher, did not succeed in laying the ghost for good."[34] Kracauer inferred from the fact that such horrifying visions cannot be dissolved that they serve no external purpose; their secret telos was not some superficial, attractive function that pointed toward a course of concrete action but instead their enshrining in memory: "The mirror reflections of horror are an end in themselves. As such they beckon the spectator to take them in and thus incorporate into his memory the real face of things too dreadful to be beheld in reality. In experiencing the rows of calves' heads [in Franju's famous documentary film about the slaughterhouse in Paris] or the litter of tortured human bodies in the films made of the Nazi concentration camps, we redeem horror from its invisibility behind the veils of panic and imagination."[35]

The description Kracauer gives of being able to perceive the "litter of tortured human bodies" is probably quite accurate. It corresponds to the images and experiences presented in the first films of concentration camps: what we see after the liberation of the camps is how the Germans who are led through the camps turn their heads away from the mountains of corpses with the most violent movements; in the cinema, they remain seated in front of the screen. Yet it is clear that Kracauer's argument does not confine itself to furthering rational understanding, but rather his theoretical line of argumentation comes up against intrinsic limits.

It is the primacy of the visual over the conceptual, of contemplation over mediation, that constitutes these intrinsic limits: "Seeing . . . is experiencing." In Kracauer's understanding, film gives an account of the visible world and enables the spectator to experience this—in keeping with how Benjamin presented film one-sidedly as the discoverer of the "visual unconscious."[36] Benjamin believes that it is "the camera with its aids" that allows us to see the visual world in film in a manner that reveals things which normally of necessity remain hidden to the eye. He states: "The camera first makes us aware of

unconscious optics the way psychoanalysis first acquaints us with unconscious impulses."[37] Here, Benjamin outlines the idea that in principle, every human being has the right to be reproduced in images, to
present him- or herself and to represent: "Any man today can lay
claim to being filmed."[38] Although Benjamin's use of this motif remains exclusively restricted to social participation in film, in the context of his idea of the visual unconscious, the cinematic presentation
of what has remained socially invisible to date also receives that redemptive quality of secular inspiration inherent in the exposure of
what is not seen.

In his essay on Benjamin in *The Mass Ornament*, Kracauer emphasized the former's theological intentions which, in the final instance,
were not so very different from his own. The idea that something
takes place "between heaven and hell, behind the backs of things,"
is an idea that would seem to gel quite well with his later notion of
the "anteroom" of history.[39] After all, at least up to and including his
Theory of Film Kracauer accorded primacy to the visual, an idea first
developed in the book on history to include redemption of the world
of things via their historiographical identification and their transformation into narration. Thus, in the end Kracauer indeed arrives
where Adorno has always believed him to be, namely in the world of
things as the only true world worthy of redemption; the visual is the
medium, not the thing itself.

Adorno painted a portrait of Kracauer, a friend of his youth, by
describing the latter's reaction to a childhood in which the relationship to things was definitely more animated than the later functional
relationship an adult has to things formed of dead material: "In Kracauer, the fixation on childhood, as a fixation on play, takes the form
of a fixation on the benignness of things; presumably the primacy of
the optical in him is not something inborn, but rather the result of this
relationship to the world of objects."[40]

Evidently, both areas do not exist as realms separated from each
other. The domain of the visual, of showing and presenting things,
merely substitutes eye contact for tactile contact with things. Benjamin discerned this quite clearly when he drew an analogy between
Surrealism and film. However, in his writings each film as a whole
becomes an animistic thing that attacks the spectator: "The work of

art of the Dadaists became an instrument of ballistics. It hit the spectator like a bullet, it happened to him, thus acquiring a tactile quality. It promoted a demand for the film, the distracting element of which is also primarily tactile, being based on changes of place and focus which periodically assail the spectator."[41]

More recent psychoanalytic approaches in film theory resort to similar experiential structures. These result from the passive stance of the audience as well as the hyperactivity on the screen, which attempts to seize hold of the spectators—a sadomasochistic symbiosis, a "fort/da" game in the sense of Freud's theory of the transitional object with which the infant playfully learns to overcome its separation anxiety by making itself into the agent of a process of permanent disappearance and reappearance.

THE PRIMACY OF THE VISUAL

If "seeing" is understood as "experiencing," then it is only possible to experience mass annihilation to the extent that we can give it visual form. Only that which is concrete in nature, that which belongs to the world of physical things, can be visualized. Kracauer innately trusts that what is immune to redemption will dissipate when transformed into images; this assumption underlies his ontological notion of the visual, of the image as the "act of the redemption of physical reality." According to Kracauer's reading of the myth of the Gorgon's head, Perseus is actually the hero *not* because he finally cuts off Medusa's head, but because he had the courage to look at her in his shield. One could easily see in such an interpretation a heretic reply to iconoclasm itself: the images one is forbidden to make of Yahweh harbor a slight redemptive glow for him who has the courage nevertheless to contemplate them.

One can judge how far Kracauer was willing to go in this respect less from the finely honed and enigmatic early prose pieces and more from the study he was commissioned to undertake in an expert capacity and in which his philosophical thoughts are voiced more brashly and boldly. In his analysis titled *Propaganda and the Nazi War Film*, carried out, as we have seen, at the Museum of Modern Art in 1942

111

with the help of a Rockefeller Foundation stipend to support psychological warfare, Kracauer examined the structure of Nazi weekly
newsreels and war reporting as well as the propagandistic function of
staged war films. Although we must assume, of course, that knowledge of Nazi films could not have been particularly comprehensive at
that time, it is nevertheless noticeable that Kracauer brings in a
strong theoretical argument with which to explain the minimal presence of anti-Semitic propaganda:

> Except for the aforementioned Polish war episode, however, these vi-
> tuperations are confined to a few hints that, unseconded by visuals, dis-
> appear in the mass of verbal statements. While the Nazis continued
> practicing, printing, and broadcasting their radical anti-Semitism, they
> reduced its role in the war films, apparently hesitant to spread it through
> pictures. On the screen, anti-Jewish activities are almost as taboo as,
> for instance, concentration camps or sterilizations. All this can be done
> and propagated in print and speech, but it stubbornly resists pictorial
> representation. The image seems to be the last refuge of violated human
> dignity.[42]

The assumption that there had to be something in the pictures themselves that disseminated a kind of holy fear of their abuse unfortu-
nately did not apply to the Nazis. They desisted neither from representing anti-Semitic propaganda pictorially, nor from having films
made in the concentration camps showing their atrocious acts. With
regard to Kracauer's writings, it is never possible to unilaterally reconcile the various strands of trenchant ideology critique—undertaken
from the perspective of "extraterritoriality"—with the unrestrained
yearning for the "suggestive power of raw material brought in by the
cameras."[43]

Although Kracauer does not, other than in the short passages on
Medusa, ask whether visual primacy has not conclusively short-
circuited as a phenomenological process, given that the events of the
death camps exceeded all that can be humanly experienced in terms
of their graphic impact, in his writings in exile it nevertheless becomes clear that he is nagged by a persistent doubt. The images on
which he as a critic often took a very unequivocal stance now become
ambiguous witnesses to the times, as if they could still hold messages

after the fact—messages which, written with invisible ink, only reveal themselves to the experienced eye.

The primacy of the visual, what Kracauer terms the redemption of reality through its pictorial representation, comes up against intrinsic limits in those areas that are to be redeemed in the image and are supposed to permit anamnestic solidarity with the dead—for they elude visual presentation in any form. The concrete quality of visual plasticity that attaches itself in film to an extant object—the image—intrinsically goes against the grain of a portrayal of the essence of *mass* destruction. What we see instead is a horrifying hierarchy extending from the mountains of corpses of those whose bodies remained to be captured on film, to the people who literally went up in smoke, having left behind them no visual mnemonic trace that could herald their redemption. It would seem to be no coincidence that Kracauer asked one of the key questions of aesthetics after Auschwitz only in passing, circuitously. Kracauer attempted to remain true to himself in according the visual primacy, although in fact it was no longer possible to pile the stones of remembrance up on top of each other. This, too, is an example of Kracauer's obstinacy.

At the End: A Philosophy
of History and Historiography

KRACAUER's *Theory of Film* was followed by *History: The Last Things before the Last,* Kracauer's last book. For him, the difference between the two subjects was marginal. He considers his defense of historiography against the truth claims made by philosophy, on the one hand, and the mathematical sciences, on the other, to be an approach similar to that used in his defense of film, a medium that, in the eyes of the phenomenologists, should remain as distant from formal art as from mere instrumentalization geared to external purposes. For, in Kracauer's view, historiography and photography furthermore have privileged access to the concrete. The image is to the redemption of the world of things what the evocation of things is to the collections and stories of the historiographer.

This process of redemptive naming takes place through reification, by apparatus-based reproduction of the pictures. If the historian wants to gain access to historical phenomena, then he has to transform himself mimetically to adapt to their petrified surface. He cannot understand alien, past life-worlds by means of operations of subsumptive logic with a view to writing a "universal history," but rather only through petrifaction, that is "self-eradication." The historiographer is someone who has been exiled from modern times, who resides in a foreign kingdom as a silent observer. As Kracauer writes, this image of the historiographer takes the exile as its model:

> I am thinking of the exile who as an adult person has been forced to leave his country or has left it of his own free will . . . and the odds are that he will never fully belong to the community to which he now in a way belongs. . . . Where then does he live? In the near-vacuum of extra-territoriality, the very no-man's-land. . . . The exile's true mode of existence is that of a stranger. . . . There are great historians who owe much of their greatness to the fact that they were expatriates. . . .

It is only in this state of self-effacement or homelessness that the historian can commune with the material of his concern. . . . A stranger to the
world evoked by the sources, he is faced with the task—the exile's task—
of penetrating its outward appearance, so that he may learn to understand
that world from within.[1]

It is not difficult to gather from this image of the historiographer how
the author sees himself, the self-portrait which we can recollect was
innate in innumerable motifs in his early essays, in brilliant, multi-
layered language. It is not surprising that the metamorphosis of petrifaction Kracauer describes as "active passivity"[2] derives from the position of the "attendants," the "passer-by," who is a "vagabond," and
that the historiographer comes to light in that position.

Kracauer's book on history is pervaded by a mood that vacillates
strangely between a strenuous avoidance of ideology and the longing
for meaning. Motifs crop up in it that had already appeared in the
essays collected in *The Mass Ornament*, yet here they gather another,
more concrete historical meaning around themselves. The longing to
assimilate to the world of mute things, to be their participant chronicler, already surfaced in the penultimate paragraph of "Farewell to
the Linden Arcade," the last of the essays: "What we had inherited
and unhesitatingly called our own lay in the passageway as if in a
morgue, exposing its extinguished grimace. In this arcade, we ourselves encountered ourselves as deceased. But we also wrested from
it what belongs to us today and forever, that which glimmered there
unrecognized and distorted."[3]

The impossibility of reconstructing history as that logical course of
chronological time that can be subsumed under a general principle
engenders the image of a discontinuous world of ruptures and rejec-
tions, whose chronicler can only be a survivor who has passed
through the cataracts of time unscathed. At this point, Kracauer returns to a "legendary" figure who already formed the title of the chapter: "Ahasuerus, or the Riddle of Time." In this figure, Kracauer sees
the lost unity as being transcended negatively. In a peculiar description he hints that the figure of the survivor is someone who is con-
demned not to die—a figure who from today's perspective reminds
us so vividly of the symptoms of the guilt of surviving that the only

115

puzzling thing about Kracauer's description is the exclusion of this connotation:

> It occurs to me that the only reliable informant on these matters, which are so difficult to ascertain, is a legendary figure—Ahasuerus, the Wandering Jew. He indeed would know firsthand the developments and transitions, for he alone in all of history has had the unsought opportunity to experience the process of becoming and decaying itself. (How unspeakably terrible he must look! To be sure, his face cannot have suffered from aging, but I imagine it to be many faces, each reflecting one of the periods which he traversed and all of them combining into ever new patterns, as he, restlessly, and vainly, tries on his wanderings to reconstruct out of the times that shaped him the one time he is doomed to incarnate.)[4]

Further on in this chapter, Kracauer addresses, as he does elsewhere, the temporal structure in Proust's "Remembrance of Things Past," which is written from a perspective he in turn amalgamates with that of the photographer who seeks aesthetic redemption through reification in the image. For Kracauer, the obstacles to the Proustian undertaking emerge in the fact that the history of the narrator's life can only be told from the viewpoint of its end; its fragmentations appear as the memory of experiences. He writes: "And the reconciliation he effects between the antithetic propositions at stake—his denial of the flow of time and his [belated] endorsement of it—hinges on his retreat into the dimension of art. But nothing of the sort applies to history. Neither has history an end, nor is it amenable to aesthetic redemption."[5]

In this passage, then, Kracauer yields to his older, rationalistic impulse by blurring the strict distinction between art and history, which he had nearly made disappear before our eyes when describing Proust's photographic view of things. He does so, however, only in order to allow the idea of redemption to arise again at a higher level. He concludes the Ahasuerus chapter with three sentences full of paradox: "The antinomy at the core of time is insoluble. Perhaps the truth is that it can be solved only at the end of Time. Proust's personal solution foreshadows, or indeed signifies, this unthinkable end—the imaginary moment at which Ahasuerus, before disintegrating, may for the first time be able to look back on his wanderings through the periods."[6]

The antinomy is "insoluble," truth "perhaps" also, for it refers to the end of time, which is "inconceivable." If the end of history arrives, Ahasuerus, the chronicler and survivor, will dissolve, for then the dead will come back to the earth. Thus in the end, Ahasuerus becomes a figure representative of something else, namely the terrible face assembled from the many faces of the dead. That unimaginable leap out of time would be redemption. Kracauer, of course, leaves this all to the realm of the imaginary.

Kracauer operates no differently in his essay "Those Who Wait," for there, in light of the decay of the old contents of faith and the resulting void and longing, he beats a skeptical retreat from the false alternative between the "principal skeptic" and the "Messianic enthusiast": "Still, in these realms every indication is certainly anything but a pointer to the path. Must it be added that getting oneself ready is only a preparation for that which cannot be obtained by force, a preparation for transformation and for giving oneself over to it? Exactly when this transformation will come to pass and whether or not it will happen at all is not at issue here, and at any rate should not worry those who are exerting themselves."[7]

With the materialist impulse of the trained architect who must pay attention to the engineering of airy constructions, in his book on history Kracauer also constructs a space that, like the anteroom of a railway station, is supposed to take in those who are waiting. The historian, he writes, settles "in an area which has the character of an anteroom. [Yet it is this 'anteroom' in which we breathe, move, and live.]"[8] The anteroom is thus our life-world, and it is here that the viewpoint from which we can put something into narrative form develops, namely from the context of concrete history. In his last book Kracauer again remains true to his unique position between phenomenology and metaphysics, just as he did in *Theory of Film*. The primacy of the optical is only relinquished in order to bring things onto a different level of mediation.

As early as the 1920s, Kracauer's own position can be described as that of an extraterritorial observer. With his distrustful stance toward any claim to systematization, he creates lucid critiques of the various attempts to cling to blind hope given the decay of the value systems and systems of belief shored up by closed intellectual edifices. The book on history follows on from this perspective. It is therefore not surprising that it casts a critical glance at all those attempts to interpret universal history as a chronological development that comprehensibly advances into a certain future. By contrast, it attaches importance to the "cataracts" of time, to those many simultaneous micro-histories that only have a meaning in the respective context in which they are experienced. There are analogies here to the more recent debate on history and histories, macro- and micro-history, the narratological problems of presenting history (against which background even the rationally justified relativistic agenda of historicism pales). However, it would be wrong therefore to conclude that Kracauer was a precursor of the postmodern critique of the link between a history of philosophy and historiography. Kracauer welcomes the loss and collapse of the major systems of religion and of promised salvation, but he by no means greets it with some new heathen fiery joy. Instead he regards the fact that they have lost their core with mixed feelings. I understand the criticism he makes less as a critique of religion in the classical sense of ideology critique and more as a critique of the functionalized substitutes. Indeed, in the 1920s he was already speaking of an artificially filled-out "empty middle."

It is no coincidence that the book on history is at the center of more recent studies of Kracauer's thought. For precisely in it do we repeatedly come across observations that concur with the way problems are seen today. For example, Kracauer emphasizes that a not inconsiderable part of the meaning generated by history depends on the language in which historiography is written and history portrayed. The historian resorts to *"formal* expedients involving structure and composition." "There is practically no general narrative that would not draw on them. What the narrator cannot accomplish in the dimension of content he expects to achieve in the aesthetic dimension."[9]

Kracauer quite clearly construes the point at which science flips over into art in historical narration in terms of a long tradition, although he immediately relativizes this. To the extent that he has already redefined his own concept of art first in *The Mass Ornament* and then in *Theory of Film*, in the book on history he revises it again when endeavoring to pinpoint a legitimate and an unjustified transgression of history into art. The legitimate occasion is encapsulated in the image of the doctor, who acts finding a diagnosis for the life-world and has the sensitivity this task requires, namely "the aesthetic sensibility of a diagnostician." History transgresses unjustifiably into art if the historical material is betrayed for aesthetic reasons. Dagmar Barnouw has attempted in her book on Kracauer's *critical realism* to define his version of the *metahistory* debate following Hayden White's approach.[10]

In many respects, it is easier to link *History: The Last Things before the Last* to the current discussion on "history vs. histories" than it is, for example, to bridge *Theory of Film* with more recent discussions in the discipline. This is perhaps so because Kracauer, as Paul Oskar Kristeller remarked in the foreword to the 1968 edition, which was based on the Kracauer Estate, "hesitates . . . to give a definitive solution, [but rather] formulates a problem and thus lays the ground for further thought."[11] The observation that Kracauer's strength lay precisely in finding critical labels for problems and dilemmas without wishing to solve them, or even being able to do so, is far more true of *History* than it is of others of Kracauer's works; after all, above all *Theory of Film* is characterized by strict positions.

Kracauer's last book, destined to remain a fragment, not only attests to how amazingly widely read he was and how open-minded he was when approaching new writers and texts. It also bears witness to his talent as an author, an ability he succeeded in maintaining even when writing in English. Karsten Witte rightly wrote: "His choice of language, specifically in English, is in many instances neither contemporary nor out-date; it appears somehow 'out of time' and also does not avoid stylistic idiosyncrasies such as archaisms, catachreses, pleonasms and paradoxes."[12]

This also evidences the inner coherence of widely scattered thoughts. Many of the motifs that Kracauer, if he did not actually discover them, at least traced and shed light on in his early writings recur and thus illuminate for readers the core thought in Kracauer's writings. On occasion, they take the form of critique, as, for example, when, with reference to historicism, he complains about Ranke as follows: "Whenever Ranke himself looks out of the window of political history to survey the neighboring regions of art, philosophy, science, etc., he insists on explaining goings-on in them from the total situation, at such and such a moment, of the nations or peoples whose destinies he narrates."[13]

The thrust of *From Caligari to Hitler* is aimed against exactly this form of causal determinism that endeavors to derive all cultural phenomena from one scheme of events. There, Kracauer turns on an approach that tries to explain an "event" in terms of cultural and sociopsychological conditions that can, instead, be quite "uncontemporaneous" sedimentation. However, if we refer Kracauer's disparate writings to one another then we soon find ourselves caught on the horns of the dilemma Kracauer attacked so vehemently and which involves coherence, and with it historical meaning, being attributed to something after the event. Kracauer writes: "And often enough the narrator's compulsive efforts to interrelate things actually miles apart result in statements which are far-fetched, to say the least."[14]

The historical distance with which more recent evaluations of Kracauer's work have been made evidently also allows the "only possible" view of the "cataract" of the history of his oeuvre in the manner in which Kracauer describes it so impressively with reference to the historical figure of Ahasuerus. Critical distance, something he held in such high regard, is perhaps the most fitting way one can address his oeuvre or, in his sense, works—they are not only disparate but all discernibly bear his intentions and his signature.

Notes

CHAPTER 1

1. Quoted in Ingrid Belke and Irina Renz, *Siegfried Kracauer: 1889–1966* (Marbach, 1988; Marbacher Magazin 47 (1988): 118.
2. Ibid., 125, illus. 55.
3. Ibid.
4. Siegfried Kracauer, *History: The Last Things before the Last*, completed by Paul Oskar Kristeller with a new preface (Princeton: Markus Wiener, 1995), 4.
5. Siegfried Kracauer, *Ginster*, in *Schriften*, ed. Karsten Witte (Frankfurt: Suhrkamp, 1973), 7:106f.
6. See Kracauer, "Die Bibel auf deutsch" (1926), in *Schriften*, ed. Inka Mülder-Bach (Frankfurt: Suhrkamp, 1990), 5.1:355.
7. Theodor W. Adorno, "The Curious Realist: Siegfried Kracauer," *New German Critique*, 54 (Fall 1991): 159–60.
8. Leo Lowenthal, "As I Remember Friedel," *New German Critique* 54 (Fall 1991): 10.
9. Ibid.
10. See Siegfried Kracauer, "Über die Freundschaft," in *Schriften*, 5.1: 27.
11. See letter from Adorno and Kracauer on Lowenthal's wedding on October 23, 1923, quoted in Lowenthal, "As I Remember Friedel," 12. The notion of "transcendental homelessness" stems from Lukács' *Theory of the Novel*, where he uses it to describe the position of the bourgeois compared with the ancient Greeks.

CHAPTER 2

1. Siegfried Kracauer, *Soziologie als Wissenschaft* (Sociology as Science), in *Schriften* (Frankfurt: Suhrkamp, 1971), 1: 14.
2. See ibid.
3. Ibid., 100.
4. Ibid., 101.
5. Ibid.
6. Inka Mülder, *Siegfried Kracauer—Grenzgänger zwischen Theorie und Literatur. Seine frühen Schriften 1913 bis 1933* (Siegfried Kracauer—Walking a tightrope between theory and literature. His early writings) (Stuttgart, 1985), 29.

7. Horkheimer to Rosa Riekher, January 30, 1921, quoted in Rolf Wiggershaus, *Die Frankfurter Schule* (The Frankfurt school) (Munich, 1986), 34.

8. Quoted in Belke and Renz, *Siegfried Kracauer: 1889–1966*, 19.

9. See Mülder, *Siegfried Kracauer*, 40.

10. Siegfried Kracauer, *Der Detektiv-Roman* (The detective novel), in *Schriften* (Frankfurt: Suhrkamp, 1971), 1: 107f.

11. Ibid., 108.

12. Ibid., 109.

13. See Walter Benjamin, "Critique of Violence," in his *Selected Writings*, ed. Marcus Bullock and Michael W. Jennings (Cambridge, Mass.: Harvard University Press, 1996), 236–52.

14. Kracauer, *Der Detektiv-Roman*, 110.

15. Ibid.

16. Jacques Derrida, "Force of Law: The 'Mystical Foundation of Authority,'" in *Deconstruction and the Possibility of Justice*, trans. Mary Quaintance, ed. Drucilla Cornell, Michel Rosenfeld, and David Gray Carlson (New York and London: Routledge, 1992), 3–67, quote on p. 36.

17. Benjamin, "Critique of Violence," 254.

18. Kracauer, *Der Detektiv-Roman*, 119.

19. Ibid., 120.

20. Ibid., 139.

21. Ibid., 147.

22. Ibid., 157.

23. Ibid., 168.

24. Ibid.

25. Ibid., 203.

26. Ibid., 202.

27. Ibid., 204.

CHAPTER 3

* Trans. note: In this chapter, as in the last, I have translated the German *Kulturkritik* as "cultural criticism." The German refers to an approach that was mainly an offspring of *Lebensphilosophie*, and is equated with Nietzsche and Dilthey. The culture of the day was primarily criticized for downplaying the irrational, instinctual basis of life.

1. Sigmund Freud, "Group Psychology," in *Civilization, Society and Religion*, Penguin Freud Library, vol. 12 (Penguin: Harmondsworth, 1991), 110.

2. Ibid., 111–12.

3. Quoted in ibid., 130.

4. Siegfried Kracauer, *The Mass Ornament: Weimar Essays*, trans. Thomas Levine (Cambridge, Mass.: Harvard University Press, 1995), 75.

5. On this, see the studies by Inka Mülder-Bach, Miriam Hansen, and others.

6. Siegfried Kracauer, "Die Denkflaeche" (Conceptual Surface), in *Schriften*, 5.1: 369. The chart is my own.

7. Ibid., 5.1: 371.

8. Miriam Hansen, "Mass Culture as Hieroglyphic Writing: Adorno, Derrida, Kracauer," *New German Critique* 56 (Spring 1992), 65.

9. Kracauer, *The Mass Ornament*, 76, 77.

10. Ibid., 78.

11. Ibid.

12. Ibid.

13. Ibid., 81.

14. Freud, "Group Psychology," 160.

15. Kracauer, *The Mass Ornament*, 84.

16. Ibid., 79.

17. Ibid., 83.

18. Siegfried Kracauer, *From Caligari to Hitler: A Psychological History of the German Film* (Princeton: Princeton University Press, 1947), 93, 94.

19. Kracauer, *Die Angestellten* (The office workers), in *Schriften*, 1: 209.

20. Ibid., 216. This brings to mind Brecht's famous adage that the photo of a factory cannot describe capitalism.

21. Ibid.

22. See Jacques Lacan, "Le seminaire sur 'la lettre volee,'" in his *Écrits* (Paris: Editions du Seuil, 1966).

23. Kracauer, *Die Angestellten*, 212.

24. Ibid., 223f.

25. Ibid., 228.

26. Ibid.

27. Hans Speier, *German White-Collar Workers and the Rise of Hitler* (New Haven: Yale University Press, 1986), 5–6. This important study by Hans Speier, a pupil of Karl Mannheim and Emil Lederer, was written in 1933 but was not published until later. Speier emigrated to the United States, where he taught at the New School for Social Research in New York. We should also mention the study undertaken by Erich Fromm and others in 1929 titled *Arbeiter und Angestellte am Vorabend des Dritten Reiches. Eine sozialpsychologische Untersuchung* (Wage-earners and salaried staff on the eve of the Third Reich. A socio-psychological study). This study was also first published in English when Fromm was in exile in the United States. In 1980, Wolfgang Bonss brought out a revised version with a foreword by Fromm at Deutscher Verlags-Anstalt. In the introduction, Bonss not only situates the study in the domain of Critical Theory, but also in relation to the empirical sociology of workers and clerical staff in the 1920s. In this study,

the specific cultural orientation of office workers is compared with that of wage laborers.

28. Kracauer, *Die Angestellten*, 283.

29. Ibid., 286.

30. Ibid., 287. Grinzing is a suburb of Vienna typical of the open-air wine gardens.

31. Quoted in Leo Lowenthal, "Literatur und Massenkultur," in Lowenthal, *Schriften* (Frankfurt: Suhrkamp, 1990), 1:11.

32. Kracauer, *Die Angestellten*, 288.

33. Patrice Petro, "Modernity and Mass Culture in Weimar: Contours of a Discourse on Sexuality in Early Theories of Perception and Representation," *New German Critique* 40 (Winter 1987): 139. See also her *Joyless Streets: Women and Melodramatic Representation in Weimar Germany* (Princeton: Princeton University Press, 1989).

34. See Sabine Hake, "Girls and Crisis: The Other Side of Diversion," *New German Critique* 40 (Winter 1987): 145–64; Emilie Altenloh, *Soziologie des Kinos* (Jena, 1914; reprint: Hamburg, 1977).

35. Heide Schlüpmann, "Kinosucht," *Frauen und Film* (Addicted to cinema) 33 (1982): 45–52.

36. See Heide Schlüpmann, "Phenomenology of Film: On Siegfried Kracauer's Writings of the 1920s," *New German Critique* 40 (Winter 1987): 100.

37. Siegfried Kracauer, "Cult of Distraction," in *The Mass Ornament*, 323–28.

CHAPTER 4

1. Siegfried Kracauer, *Ginster*, in *Schriften*, ed. Karsten Witte (Frankfurt: Suhrkamp, 1973), 7: 192.

2. Ibid., 158.

3. Ibid., 122.

4. Ibid., 123.

5. Ibid., 192.

6. Ibid.

7. Ibid.

8. Ibid.

9. Ibid., 102.

10. Ibid., 102f.

11. Ibid., 124.

12. See Eckhardt Köhn, "Die Konkretionen des Intellekts" (The concretions of the intellect), *Text + Kritik* 68 (1980): 47.

13. Martin Seel, "Am Beispiel der Metapher. Zum Verhältnis von buchstäblicher und figürlicher Rede" (The example of the metaphor. On the relation of literal to figurative speech), in *Forum für Philosophie Bad Homburg*,

ed. Intentionalitaet und Verstehen (Frankfurt, 1990), 248. Perspective as a conceptual concept played a key role for Kracauer in all his thought, and not only for his film theory. On this, see above all the discussion in his *History: The Last Things before the Last*.

14. This is the claim by Rolf Wiggershaus in his essay "Ein abgrundtiefer Realist. Die Aktualisierung des Marxismus und das Institut für Sozialforschung" (A profoundly deep realist. The up-dating of Marxism and the Institut für Sozialforschung), in Siegfried Kracauer: Neue Interpretationen, ed. Michael Kessler and Thomas Y. Levin (Stauffenberg, 1990), 285.

15. Kracauer, *Ginster*, 177.

16. Ibid., 233.

17. Ibid., 232.

18. Joseph Roth, "Wer ist Ginster?" (Who is Ginster?), in *Frankfurter Zeitung*, literary supplement, November 25, 1928. Quoted in Belke and Renz, *Siegfried Kracauer: 1889–1966*, 52. On the reception of the book at the time, see the afterword by the editor of *Frankfurter Zeitung*, Karsten Witte.

19. Kracauer, *Ginster*, 242.

20. Inka Mülder-Bach, "Schlupfloecher. Die Diskontinuitaet des Kontinuierlichen im Werk Siegfried Kracauers," in Kessler and Levin, *Siegfried Kracauer*, 255.

21. Quoted in Karsten Witte, "Nachwort" (Postscript), in *Schriften*, 7: 506.

22. Thomas Mann to Kracauer, December 8, 1934, in *Schriften*, 7:505.

23. Kracauer, *Ginster*, 21.

24. Ibid., 84.

25. Siegfried Kracauer, *Georg*, in *Schriften*, 7: 261f.

26. Kracauer, *Ginster*, 21.

27. Kracauer, *Georg*, 278.

28. Ibid., 398.

29. Ibid., 399.

30. Ibid., 398f.

31. Ibid., 411.

32. Charles Bernheimer, "Manets Olympia: der Skandal auf der Leinwand" (Manet's Olympia. The scandal on canvas), in *Weiblichkeit als Maskerade* (Femininity as masquerade), ed. Lilliane Weissberg (Frankfurt, 1994), 155.

33. On this, see Heide Schlüpmann, "Der Gang ins Kino—ein Ausgang aus selbstverschuldeter Unmuendigkeit. Zum Begriff des Publikums in Kracauers Essayistik der Zwanziger Jahre," in Kessler and Levin, *Siegfried Kracauer*, pp. 267–84. Schlüpmann emphasizes in particular the homosexual aspects and the female presence as a factor disturbing Kracauer.

34. Ernst Kris and Otto Kurz, *Die Legende vom Kuenstler. Ein geschicht-*

licher Versuch (The legend of the artist. A historical study) (1934: reprint, Frankfurt, 1995), 164. In this study (Ernst Kris later made a name for himself as a theorist in the field of psychoanalysis), the focus is on the reconstruction of the patterns in biographical interpretations of legendary artists in the applied arts and the mythical projections of a culture onto the artists in question that these evidence.

35. Siegfried Kracauer, *Offenbach and the Paris of His Time*, trans. Gwenda David and Eric Mosbacher (London: Constable and Co., 1937), 60.

36. Ibid., 59.

37. The entire correspondence between Adorno and Benjamin on Kracauer's book is found in Theodor W. Adorno and Walter Benjamin, *Briefwechsel 1928–1940* (Frankfurt: Suhrkamp, 1994), 204–52, quoted on pp. 243–44.

38. Kracauer, *Offenbach* (my translation). The official translation gives the erroneous reading: "Fear of being driven from the safe, familiar world must certainly have intensified his homesickness" (35).

39. Ibid., 10.

40. Ibid. (My translation in italics; the central passage is on p. 146 of the translation.

41. See Katherine Woods, "Offenbach and the Paris of His Time," *New York Review of Books*, March 27, 1938, p. 5.

42. Kracauer, *Offenbach*, 152.

43. Jean-Paul Sartre, *The Family Idiot: Gustav Flaubert, 1821–1857*, vol. 1, trans. Carol Cosman (Chicago: University of Chicago Press, 1981). The five-volume French original was published in Paris in 1972.

44. Ibid., x.

45. Ibid.

46. Kracauer, Offenbach (Gaines: my translation).

47. See ibid., 344.

48. Ibid., 340.

CHAPTER 5

1. Siegfried Kracauer, "Über die Aufgabe des Filmkritikers" (On the task of the film critic), in his *Kino. Essay, Studien, Glossen zum Film, ed. Karsten Witte* (Frankfurt: Suhrkamp, 1974), 6:11.

2. Oral communication from Annette Michelson, New York University.

3. Kracauer, *Caligari*, 11.

4. Ibid.

5. Ibid., 10.

6. See ibid., 10nn. 20–23.

7. See Erich Fromm, *Gesamtausgabe*, vol. 3 (Stuttgart, 1980).

8. Ibid., 8.

9. Kracauer, *Caligari*, 9.

10. Ibid., 7.

11. Ibid.

12. Ibid., 6.

13. Ibid. The quote comes from Erwin Panofsky's essay, published in different versions since 1936, "On Movies" (1936), "Style and Medium in the Motion Pictures," (1947). The essay first appeared in German in *Filmkritik*, 11 (1967): 343–55; reprinted in Erwin Panofsky, *Die ideologischen Vorläufer des Rolls-Royce-Kühlers* (The ideological precursor of the Rolls-Royce radiator grill) (Frankfurt, 1993). The volume also includes two essays on Panofsky, which contain historical and biographical background material. Panofsky, who was a passionate cinema-goer, originally presented his hypotheses in the form of a lecture to a group of film-lovers in Princeton who wished to found a film archive attached to the Museum of Modern Art. The version Kracauer quotes first came out in 1937 in *Transition*, a Paris journal that appeared in English. On the intellectual friendship between Kracauer and Panofsky and its influence on Kracauer see Volker Breidecker, "Kracauer und Panofsky. Ein Rencontre im Exil" (Kracauer and Panofsky. An encounter in exile), in *Im Blickfeld. Jahrbuch der Hamburger Kunsthalle. Konstruktion der Moderne*, ed. Hamburger Kunsthalle (Hamburg, 1994), 125–47 and the correspondence announced for publication in 1996, edited by Breidecker.

14. Kracauer, *Caligari*, 7.

15. Ibid., 21.

16. Ibid., 88.

17. Ibid., 91.

18. Ibid., 166.

19. Ibid., 214.

20. Ibid., 272.

21. Siegfried Kracauer to Erwin Panofsky, December 17, 1943, quoted in Breidecker, "Kracauer und Panofsky," 139.

22. On this, see Breidecker, "Kracauer und Panofsky."

23. Kracauer, *Caligari*, 249–50.

24. Hermann G. Weinberg, "The Film Humanity," *Sight and Sound* 16 (Summer, 1946): 78f.

25. On this point, see my book *Die Einstellung ist die Einstellung. Visuelle Konstruktionen des Judentums* (The Angle is the attitude. Visual constructions of Jewry) (Frankfurt, 1992), in particular the section "Die Kritische Theorie in Hollywood"(Critical theory in Hollywood), 54–126.

26. Martha Wolfenstein and Nathan Leites, untitled, in the "Book reviews" section of the *Psychoanalytic Quarterly*, April 16, 1947, p. 570.

27. Siegfried Kracauer, "Hollywood's Terror Films: Do They Reflect an American State of Mind?" *Commentary* 2 (1946): 132–36.

28. Ibid., 133.

29. On the subcutanean foundations of Kracauer's thought by mass destruction, see the final chapter of this book.

30. See Siegfried Kracauer, "Das Grauen im Film," *Neue Zürcher Zeitung*, April 25, 1940, quoted in *Kino*, 25–27. See also Miriam Hansen, "Dinosaurier sehen und nicht gefressen werden: Kino als Ort der Gewaltwahrnehmung bei Benjamin, Kracauer und Spielberg," in *Auge und Affekt. Wahrnehmung und Interaktion* (Eye and election. Perception and interaction), in Gertrud Koch, ed. (Frankfurt, 1995), 249–71.

31. Wolfenstein and Leites, untitled, 571.

32. The worst history of the reception of Kracauer's study were not the objections that it was Marxist, one-sided, teleological, psychoanalytical, mystical, or somehow unsuitable, but was rather the overall reception of the book in Germany. There, it appeared only in a truncated, censored edition. When it did finally come out in a full edition, hardly a single reviewer bothered to present more than general objections against sociological thought, social psychology, and ideology critique. On the German reception and the book's German publication history, see Karsten Witte's "Nachwort der Herausgebers" in the German edition.

33. Mark Ferro, "Gibt es eine filmische sicht der Geschichte?" (Is there a filmic view of history?), in *Bilder schreiben Geschichte. Der Historiker im Kino* (Images write history. The historian in the cinema), in Rainer Rother, ed. (Berlin, 1991), 24.

CHAPTER 6

1. Quoted in Belke and Renz, *Siegfried Kracauer, 1889–1966*, 107.

2. Ibid. "During the months spent in fear and misery in Marseilles, I made longer notes on the subject." Miriam Hansen has meanwhile taken these "notes" as the basis for a new reading of *Theory of Film*, with the express intention of using such a "historicization" to uncover the roots of the *Theory of Film* and thus generate a new interpretation that re-creates the tension between the earlier poignant insights and the rounded text of the book that was finally published—with a sort of processual, intertextual reading. See Miriam Hansen, "With Skin and Hair: Kracauer's Theory of Film, Marseilles 1940," *Critical Inquiry* 3, no. 19 (Spring 1993): 437–69. The essay is part of a larger project: the first systematic study on works on film and mass culture prepared by persons in or around the Frankfurt School. To this extent, the methodological approach used, namely historicization, should be seen as part of a comprehensive presentation intended to further the history of ideas.

3. See Dagmar Barnouw, *Critical Realism: History, Photography and the World of Siegfried Kracauer* (Baltimore and London, 1994). Barnouw criti-

cizes the attempts by Miriam Hansen and David Rodowick to understand Kracauer in the context of the thought of Walter Benjamin; in her own work, she unravels Kracauer's notion of realism strongly in keeping with the theory of photography of the time.

4. Adorno to Benjamin, February 29, 1940, in Adorno and Benjamin, *Briefwechsel, 1928–1940*, 417.

5. Siegfried Kracauer, "Photography," in *The Mass Ornament*, 47.

6. Ibid., 48.

7. Ibid., 50.

8. Ibid., 59, quoted in Johann Jakob Bachofen, *Oknos der Seilflechter*, ed. Manfred Schroeter (Munich, 1923).

9. Ibid., 59.

10. Ibid.

11. Ibid., 60.

12. Ibid., 60–61.

13. Ibid., 61.

14. Ibid., 62.

15. Ibid.

16. On this, see Rudolf Arnheim's exhaustive review of the Kracauer book. He refers to Kracauer's emphasis on the "material evidence." Arnheim, "Melancholy Unshaped," *Journal for Aesthetics and Art Criticism* 213 (Spring 1963): 292.

17. Siegfried Kracauer, *Theory of Film: The Redemption of Physical Reality* (London: Oxford University Press, 1960), ix.

18. Ibid., x.

19. Thierry de Duve, "Time Exposure and Snapshot: The Photograph as Paradox," *October* 5 (Summer 1978): 115.

20. Kracauer, *Theory of Film*, xi.

21. Hansen, "With Skin and Hair."

22. Kracauer, *Theory of Film*, 158.

23. Ibid., 165.

24. Ibid., 40.

25. Ibid., 44.

26. Ibid., 56–57.

27. Ibid., 77.

28. Ibid, 300.

29. Kracauer, *History*, 201.

30. Ibid., 233.

31. Ibid., 136.

32. Kracauer, *Theory of Film*, 305.

33. Ibid.

34. Ibid.

35. Ibid., 306.

36. Walter Benjamin, "The Work of Art in the Age of Mechanical Reproduction," in his *Illuminations*, trans. Harry Zohn (Glasgow: Jonathan Cape, 1970), 219–54.

37. Ibid., 239.

38. Ibid., 233.

39. See Siegfried Kracauer, "On the Writings of Walter Benjamin," in *The Mass Ornament*, 262.

40. Theodor W. Adorno, "The Curious Realist: On Siegfried Kracauer," *New German Critique* 54 (Fall 1991): 159–77, quote on p. 177.

41. Benjamin, "The Work of Art," 240.

42. Kracauer, *Caligari*, 304–5.

43. Kracauer, *Theory of Film*, 302.

CHAPTER 7

1. Kracauer, *History*, 83–84.

2. Ibid., 85.

3. Siegfried Kracauer, "Farewell to the Linden Arcade," in *The Mass Ornament*, 337–42, quote on p. 342.

4. Kracauer, *History*, 157.

5. Ibid., 163.

6. Ibid.

7. Siegfried Kracauer, "Those Who Wait," in *The Mass Ornament*, 129–40, quote on p. 140.

8. Kracauer, *History*, 195.

9. Ibid., 175.

10. See Barnouw, "Critical Realism." See also her contribution to Kessler and Levin, *Siegfried Kracauer*.

11. Paul Oskar Kristeller, foreword, in Kracauer, *History*, xiv.

12. Karsten Witte, postscript to the German edition of *History* which he translated in: *Geschichte—Vor den letzten Dingen, Schriften*, ed. and trans. by Karsten Witte (Frankfurt: Suhrkamp, 1971), 4: 289.

13. Kracauer, *History*, 173.

14. Ibid., 174.

Bibliography

1. Works by Siegfried Kracauer

Kracauer's *The Schriften* (Collected works) has been brought out by Suhr-kamp in Frankfurt and comprises eight volumes:

Volume 1: *Soziologie als Wissenschaft; Der Detektiv-Roman; Die Ange-stellten*, 1971.

Volume 2: *Von Caligari zu Hitler*. Ed. Karsten Witte, trans. Ruth Baumgarten and Karsten Witte, 1979.

Volume 3: *Theorie des Films. Die Errettung der äußeren Wirklichkeit*. Trans. Friedrich Walter and Ruth Zellschan. Revised by the author, 1973.

Volume 4: *Geschichte—Vor den letzten Dingen*. Ed. and trans. Karsten Witte, 1971.

Volume 5.1: *Aufsätze. (1915–1926)*. Ed. Inka Mülder-Bach, 1990.

Volume 5.2: *Aufsätze. (1927–1931)*. Ed. Inka Mülder-Bach, 1990.

Volume 5.3: *Aufsätze.(1932–1965)*. Ed. Inka Mülder-Bach, 1990.

Volume 6: *Aufsätze zum Film*, forthcoming. It will include *Kino. Essays, Studien, Glossen zum Film*. Ed. Karsten Witte, 1974.

Volume 7: *Ginster; Georg*. Ed. Karsten Witte, 1973.

Volume 8: *Jacques Offenbach und das Paris seiner Zeit*. Ed. Karsten Witte, 1976.

From Caligari to Hitler: A Psychological History of the German Film. Princeton: Princeton University Press, 1947.

History: The Last Things before the Last. Completed by Paul Oskar Kristeller with a new preface. Princeton: Markus Wiener, 1995.

The Mass Ornament: Weimar Essays. Trans. Thomas Levine. Cambridge, Mass.: Harvard University Press, 1995.

Offenbach and the Paris of His Time. Trans. Gwenda David and Eric Mosbacher. London: Constable and Co., 1937. The translation is incomplete and erroneous in many respects.

Kracauer's papers are housed in Deutsche Literaturarchiv in Marbach. The estate held there includes diaries, an extensive correspondence, notebooks, manuscripts, excerpts, drawings, and drafts, as well as countless newspaper articles.

2. Letters

Benjamin, Walter. *Briefe an Siegfried Kracauer*. Ed. Theodor W. Adorno Archive. Stuttgart, 1988; *Marbacher Schriften*, 27.
Breidecker, Volker. ed. *Briefe Panovsky-Kracauer*. Berlin, 1996.

3. Bibliographies

Levin, Thomas Y. "Kracauer in English: A Bibliography," *New German Critique* 40 (1987); see also his "The English-Language Reception of Kracauer's Work: A Bibliography," *New German Critique* 54 (1991).
————. *Siegfried Kracauer. Eine Bibliographie seiner Schriften*. Marbach, 1989.
Soziographie 7, nos. 1–2, 8–9 (1994).

4. Works on Kracauer

Monographs

Barnouw, Dagmar. *Critical Realism: History, Photography and the World of Siegfried Kracauer*. Baltimore and London, 1994.
Belke, Ingrid, and Irina Renz. *Siegfried Kracauer: 1889–1966*. Marbach, 1988; *Marbacher Magazin* 47 (1988).
Mülder, Inka. *Siegfried Kracauer—Grenzgänger zwischen Theorie und Literatur. Seine frühen Schriften 1913 bis 1933*. Stuttgart, 1985.

Chapters in Books

Frisby, David. *Fragments of Modernity*. Cambridge, Mass.: MIT Press, 1986.
Jay, Martin. *Permanent Exiles: Essays on the Intellectual Migration from Germany to America*. New York, 1986; see chap. 11: "The Exterritorial Life of Siegfried Kracauer"; chap. 12: "Politics of Translation: Siegfried Kracauer and Walter Benjamin on the Buber-Rosenzweig Bible"; chap. 13: "Adorno and Kracauer: Notes on a Troubled Friendship."

Volumes of Essays

Kessler, Michael, and Thomas Y. Levin, eds. *Siegfried Kracauer. Neue Interpretationen*. Stauffenberg, 1990.

Special Issues of Journals

New German Critique 54 (1991). "Special issue on Siegfried Kracauer."
Text + Kritik 68 (1980), *Siegfried Kracauer*, a collection of essays on Kracauer.

Index

133